TAILPIECES

A Quirky Look at Life

USHI KAK

INDIA · SINGAPORE · MALAYSIA

ISBN 979-8-88815-660-5

Dedication

To my 'doubly' loveable twins, Swanzal & Himaal

Contents

Full Disclosure

'Preface' has a ring of gravitas, not very apt for a small book like this.

To instead call it 'Full disclosure' also serves the purpose of *mea culpa.* Wordsmiths must confess to a fatal fascination for punning at the drop of a word, and that remains an incurable syndrome.

This booklet is an anthology of short essays and occasional pieces, written over a period of 24 years. To my surprise most continue to have traction. Some of these featured as 'middles' on the editorial pages of national newspapers and some appeared as tail-pieces (and thereby hangs a tale!). The more recent have appeared in online magazines.

They represent my way of looking at life, in its varied hues and in a lighter vein, through global issues, language, gender equality and how tech-wizardry impacts our lives. These are the five themes that tie the pieces together.

My aspirations as a writer are best reflected by Ernest Hemingway's comment on writing:

"For a long time now I have tried to simply write the best I can. Sometimes I have good luck and I write better than I can".

Full Disclosure

Writing these has been a joyous and a healing experience for me. If these evoke even a smidgeon of joy and empathy in readers, my writing would have served its purpose.

– Ushi Kak

Digital Tectonics:
Tech Wizardry

?!
YOU ARE
> DELETED <
©Shailendra .20

Cyber Nirvana

A Mouse Click Away!

"Mom," declared my daughter one fine morning, "you should become computer literate". I chewed on this advice wondering if this would turn out to be a 'byte' too big to tackle. But the thought of being witness to the birth of a new millennium when 'infotech' would reign supreme urged me to pick up the gauntlet. Amongst the many spin-offs of this new literacy, I was assured, would be to make my occasional editorial forays a cake-walk. This was my window of opportunity. Luck comes knocking at 'windows' not at doors in this cyber-world. And, of course, for those supremely lucky, it opens the 'gates' of fortune a la Bill Gates.

A nifty demo of computer wizardry by my architect daughter, who reeled off names like Auto-Cad, 3-D, Clip-Art etc., left me in a moronic stupor. Even innocuous words like mouse, menu-bar, virus etc. overhauled my old-fashioned vocabulary, and took on a new meaning. We, mere mortals, may fall prey to viruses, but this sturdy contraption had anti-virus properties built inside. So with a degree of awe I tackled my friendly PC.

I gingerly learnt to handle the 'mouse' so as to keep the cursor from vanishing off the screen. The feather-touch keyboard typed 'tttthree' letters at my slightest gawky tap and gave me all 'CAPITALS' at times. Delete and Backspace keys that gobbled up letters like a hungry monster seemed rather violent to me. I missed the pleasure of erasing a mistake vigorously on paper with an unassuming rubber with no high-tech pretensions!

There were many more hard lessons to be learnt. Not saving a page, after a painstaking one-finger typing effort, made me realise the true meaning of love's labour lost. Just when I was beginning to get a chip on my shoulder against this wonder-chip gadget, deliverance came in the form of a heavy tome. "Microsoft Word for Dummies" must have been written with people like me in mind. It is an easy step-by-step guide book that restored my faith in my ability to unravel the mysteries of this electronic wonder.

Of course, I had no illusions of joining the tribe of computer nerds trying to crack the "Y2K" impasse before the year 2000 was upon us. But I reluctantly admitted to myself that, after all, there is a brighter side to computers. What nearly bowled me over was the cartoon Office Assistant in the garb of Einstein that popped up now and then on the screen to take down commands. Like Aladdin's magic lamp, I could summon this intellectual genie at the click of a mouse and send it packing at will.

I was almost beginning to savour the pleasures of an automatic Spelling and Grammar check when I was brought back to reality with a thud. Having typed an article when I put it through a spell-check— 'Ushi' was underlined in red with the terse comment, 'Not in Dictionary.' The cheeky machine had wiped off my very existence. I don't quite enjoy the idea of 'nirvana' through computers!

Modem, Madam

No Escape from this Bionic Nerd

It is thanks to the exhortations of my computer-savvy architect daughter that I have become computer literate. However I still keep complaining about some of the irritants in handling this bionic nerd. For one it is a nagging interlocutor. When you simply want to shut it off, it confronts you with a smart-alecky query, 'Are you sure you want to shut down the computer?' That seems to be a subtle dig at our vacillating minds. Quite often when you exit from your programme, the monitor displays dire warnings about files getting lost. I thought that happened only in the labyrinthine office interiors.

For someone who thought that an answering machine was a dreadful put-off, the brave new world of computers and internet has taken a great deal of getting used to. Like a reluctant debutante, I have been brought F2F (face to face) with the cyber world. My daughter believes, like Remo Fernandez, that one has to be a 'cyber-viber' or else remain a cipher. So her contribution to adult literacy is to make me e-literate. The modem looms large on my horizon. Surfing the Net is not easy as pie, as I was told.

Having logged on, the first hurdle was filling the user-name box. To my amazement, I could not use my name as it is, because there were 34 clones of the same name on the internet. The silly machine made me feel like an impersonator. E-mail, the new cyber-postman, delivers messages in a trice and confirms delivery instantly at the click of a mouse. None of the heartaches of sending letters via 'snail mail'—or so I thought. Having composed some of my messages in Word I tried transferring them to the internet through 'Copy' and 'Paste.' Not having clicked inside the message box, a few of my friends received blank messages. But then if you are a pro you can send e-greetings in a bouquet of colours with catchy and appropriate tunes.

There is apparently a whole new world with cyber malls, book marts, chat rooms etc. It seems anything from a book to a bride can be downloaded from the Net. What bothers me is that this machine exhibits an acute attention deficit syndrome. There isn't just the dot.com, there is also a shot. com. The moment you leave your keyboard for a short break the screen savers start cascading down the screen. They fade in and fade out in pixels, in slatted lines, top down, bottom up, side to side and what have you. Like a tempting seductress, the internet is ensnaring more and more people in its world wide web. The world is awash with cyber- speak.

The internet acolytes make you feel almost guilty if you are not a netizen. From e-poetry to e-commerce the canvas of the 'www' is painted in varied colours. From the neighbourhood *paanwala* with a website to even a cyber-beggar who thought of raising a million dollars through asking for a mere one dollar contribution on the Net— the possibilities seem mind-boggling!

***

Tech-Challenged

Reboot Oldies or else Be Logged Out

Despite Aldous Huxley's clairvoyant warning of a 'Brave New World', I must confess, at the risk of being branded a Luddite, that with all this tech-wizardry the 'Gen-Old' is quite gob-smacked! One sees even four-year old kids tapping the computer keys with the panache of a concert pianist giving a bravura performance. We struggle with our one- finger tapping of the key-board. The clichéd generation gap has morphed into a 'technology-gap' with the information revolution. One erroneously thought that learning to handle a desktop PC was cyber-nirvana. But now new technological innovation is thrown at you with jaw-dropping speed of an Ashish Nehra ball.

Going from huge main-frames to smaller computers and from there to desktops and lap-tops was dazzling enough. But now lean and mean machines, devised by digital '*wunder-kind,* challenge all notions of size zero. In addition the mind-boggling connectivity created by the Silicon Valley nerds and their ilk makes us wonder at the way the new young minds have taken to the new reality of cyber primacy like a duck to water.

We certainly need to reboot our CPU's to make sense of the world around us. There are some archaic souls amongst us who have not gone beyond the belief that a simple calculator is a marvel of technology. Yet, despite being chronologically challenged some of the oldies are forward- looking and do not show signs of tech-phobia. But members of this breed could be counted on the finger-tips. For Gen Next, however, it is the World- Wide -Web that has 'virtually' proved to be a seductive tool, one that ensnares with its instant connectivity. If you are not engaged in social networking on Facebook, Orkut, Twitter, You Tube or suchlike—you are so yesterday. What with 'convergence technology' the phone is a computer and the computer can be a phone! It makes the older generation feel very schizophrenic.

But the net-nerds are 'ideating' constantly to generate money-spinning software that could make even Midas blush. Bill Gates has his 'window' on the world. Mark Zuckerberg, the creator of the social networking site, 'Facebook', has hit such pay-dirt that he can donate a hundred million dollars without batting an eyelid. But the downside is that you may chirp and twit but Twitter it was that led to the undoing of a minister. And the upside is that even Aung San Suu Kyi wants to get on Twitter to connect with the young after a decade spent under stoic house arrest.

The revelation of some classified information on the Wikipedia has led to a lot of skeletons rattling in the closet, threatening to come out. But, at the same time, this development enhances the right to information. Besides, who can forget that internet was Barack Obama's main weapon in his brilliant presidential campaign for spreading the Democrats' word and garnering support. Maybe the tech-phobes could draw inspiration from him and believe in that catchy slogan, 'Yes we can'. Only, all this new gadgetry of 'Tablets', iPhones, iPods, et all, has played havoc with my speaking ability. And grappling with the new 'vocab' on the net makes me want to go into 'rehab'. The mountain of tech-tonic stuff makes me wonder if I have an 'Intel' inside my brain. It's bad enough we have to figure out 'Bluetooth' till we are blue in the face. To cloud my vision further is all this talk of cloud computing services.

As if matters were not confounding enough, there is an Indian whiz-kid in the US who has devised a 'sixth sense' technology (watch out Night Shyamalan!) that yields information through sheer movement of fingers. Our Hindu Gods assumed 'avatars' to rescue mankind in times of trouble but 'virtual' avatars, it seems, are all for individual salvation. My personal invocation is 'Hey RAM'! Keep me logged on somehow till the Supreme Service Provider presses the 'Delete' button on me.

✸✸✸

What's Up?

App-ropriately Caught in the World Wide Web

It's a 'Mobile' mob out there hankering for more! 'What's up?' is a good query but the question, to be more 'app-ropriate', is what's App? The virtual world is virtually impossible to ignore. The invention of the World Wide Web in the 90's by an unsuspecting Brit has created an amazing spider- web of connectivity. There are blogs of every shade and theme with interesting names to boot. Then there are micro-blogs a la Twitter (which is causing a flutter in the dove cotes in our blogosphere currently). A whole new internet related vocabulary has been minted— 'download', 'upload', 'podcast', 'blogging', 'weblog' etc. Those of us not fed on a diet of computers are zapped by the new digital vocab. It will take us a while to reconfigure the new usage, having been used to 'Baba log', Hum Log', aviator's Log Book or plain-old logs of wood. We were citizens first and 'netizens' was unheard of. Now the social media sites are the hip and happening places. You don't have a face if you are not on Face Book and if you don't see You Tube you might as well go down the tube. As for not having a handle on Twitter, you've got to be a silly twit! Not born with the new tech-savvy DNA this information overload is bound to cause a short-circuit and a burn out in our befuddled minds.

Product innovation reigns supreme now and 'apps' are the name of the game. Ask the behemoths in the digital world. Apple is truly an 'appy' happy set-up. It is *Khiladi* No. 1 in the applications segment. Steve Jobs knew his job well in tempting you to take a bigger 'byte' out of the partially chomped luscious red apple. Microsoft, the other big game player, is shedding Hotmail to have a better 'Outlook' from windows.

Apps creators must be adept in human psychology and advertising acumen. There is an Android application called 'ice-cream sandwich' for multi-tasking, and there are 'cookies' one can't bite. Apps have become 'app-endages' one can't function without. An American woman, obviously afflicted with indecision, has devised an application that helps one decide, "Should I Break Up with My Boyfriend"? App-arently, (no getting away from apps) it gives you a more accurate and statistically tested answer. Despite Barak Obama's outcry against outsourcing, even parenting is being 'outsourced' to an app called 'Chore Monster'! It tells you how to discipline kids with brattish behaviour. A news item just blew me away the other day. An app being developed called "iBrain" would map Stephen Hawking's neural pathways to convert them into speech. What worries me though is that when applied to lesser mortals, the secret will be out that it is 'head piece filled with straw' to use T.S.Eliot's phrase.

Robotics and artificial intelligence are taking on some of the difficult or dirty tasks. There is an automated household cleaning device already being advertised in the print media that is programmed to sense obstacles (unlike some of our temperamental and blundering maids), finish the sweeping and swabbing at any time you set it to. A boon for any woman! There is convergence on the horizon. Fridges will play music and alert us when we are about to run out of a certain food item. Smart homes, smart phones, smart machines, driverless cars that talk to each other without road rage! We'd better wake up and smell the coffee as there is no room for unsmart humans. Touch screens, voice-activated gadgets (what happens on days when you have a bad throat or is it a pre-recorded voice signature?).

Having straddled the world from the era of rotary phones to the gizmo-crazy world of today, I have a dreadful thought cropping up in my mind now and then— with our dependency on 'apps' and 'maps' I may have to Google the GPS device on my smart phone to find my way home!

Toolkit Strikes Again!

A Spanner in the Works

Nobody but nobody can perhaps upstage Kim Kardashian in trending topics! But lately #toolkit has been clawing its way up on the trending ladder. The hash symbol #started around 1988 to group similar messages and topics for ease of finding information in pre-Twitter era. The first Twitter hashtag was put on the net in August 2007 for the same reason and the rest is history.

The hashtag made its presence felt a decade ago in the #Occupy Wall Street protests. #Me Too began as an awareness raising platform against sexual exploitation but gained momentum post Weinstein exposé. It reared its head in Hong Kong street movement of 2019 and unarmed George Floyd's being choked to death gave a breath of life to #Black Lives Matter campaign. Up close, our anti-CAA protests showed the power of protests as a potent weapon through hashtag mobilising. #Shaheen Bagh echoed around the globe. Bilkees Bano, the gritty 82 year old Dadi of Shaheen Bagh, made it to the list of *Time* magazine's100 most influential women in the world.

From the days of yore when pamphleteering, stringing up banners, pasting posters and soapbox speeches, it sure is a quantum leap to use the digital toolkit to promote whatever your cause or streamline your work model. The thrills and spills of internet can make you a global icon or land you in prison. Greta Thunberg has repeatedly rapped the global community on the knuckles at World Economic Forum at Davos and at the U.N. by speaking the naked truth about the imminent disaster lurking around the corner for planet Earth.

A 'mere school girl' with ADHD syndrome pleading with learned leaders to press the panic button because 'our house is on fire'.

She urged them not to resort to statistical jugglery to fudge facts. This should be more than a wake up call. It is a siren sounding loud and clear! Our own young climate activist Disha Ravi was in the clink for disseminating the Thunberg #Toolkit in support of the farmers protest. Since the Delhi police couldn't lay its hands on Thunberg and Rihanna, the singer from Barbados, Disha Ravi was easy prey. Rihanna would've thumbed her nose at the cops by singing her song, 'Good girl, gone bad'!

The current #Congress-toolkit on social media is a mud slinging tug -of -war that has given oxygen to the hashtag. The humble toolkit/tool bag carried by workers worth their salt has assumed a digital avatar. Looking at the flurry of accusations flying thick and fast, #toolkit may play catch-up with the oft invoked 'foreign hand' in the pre-internet era. We, the hapless witnesses, are fully vaccinated against such 'word-salvos'. There has to be a word for this— Shashi Tharoor, please oblige!

***

Talk the Walk

Digital Perils

'Spyware' unleashed on unsuspecting individuals globally is a political hot potato these days. But in India snooping devices of the flying horse a la Pegasus variety or a more earthbound quadruped are simply a monumental waste of taxpayer's money

Yes, the title is a deliberate reading of the idiom backwards. No uber technology is required to gather information secretly. We Indians strut it all out unabashedly in our decibel declarations in public now.

Mobiles upturned the public profile of Indians like nothing before. From a deadpan visage in public to a 'mobile' face—with flashing eyes and quicksilver expressions—most Hindustanis could graduate *summa cum laude* for their *'abhinay'* from a dance school. And brought up on dramatic dialogues from Bollywood, the '*Aam Aadmi*' and '*Aam Aurat*' are able to converse with stentorian voices leaving no choice to people around to listen in or carry earmuffs.

It is not a walk in the park anymore—in more ways than one! One can not hoof around the park to find a haven of quiet amidst Nature. It feels as if one is listening to public confessions on the trot. These mobile aficionados of all ages pour their joy, anger or sorrow with such bravura. To hear the range of their topics which vary with age and the cards dealt to the individual by fate, is a revelation, sometimes as spicy as the Indian 'Magic Masala' chips!

With Covid and its cohorts cavorting around the globe playing hide and seek, humans are more than ever dependent on their devices to seek connectivity with each other. In the current battle of hide and seek between the Corona virus and the human hosts, social distancing has forced us to hunker down in our homes. WFH (work from home) or online teaching would've been unthinkable without our able digital gadgets. 'Nomo' (no mobile) is a valid syndrome. Like the mask on the bridge of the nose (quite a few use it more as a chin base!), the mobile in hand is all pervasive. A pale imitation of our Indian Gods and Goddesses with their impressive array of hand-held objects.

A mobile, despite being a treasured gadget that has empowered the less privileged in small pockets, highlights the stark inequality in digital power and knowledge.

From a simple basic device to diamond -encrusted customised mobiles for the uber rich, to futuristic devices like Google glasses or even chips under the skin, high-tech has given it many avatars. Those of us who have seen a curve from telephone exchanges, to landline, to cordless et al, the current scene looks a bit surreal. 'Future Shock' envisaged by Alvin Toffler way back in 1970 is here and now for the old generation. A host of heavyweight thinkers and scientists like Ray Kurtzweil, Yuval Noah Harare, Stephen Hawking, Nick Bostrom to Elon Musk have talked of the perils of unbridled growth of AI.

With Artificial Intelligence gaining ground steadily what's the fate of our natural intelligence! Homo Sapiens may lose their agency to machines as some futurologists fear in not too distant a future. With AI enabled rogue robots in an apocalyptic breaking out could actually lead to '*deus ex machina*' become a reality. Except the 'deus' in this case is not a saviour but has satanic intentions of eliminating the human creator. Homo Sapiens would have pressed the self-destruct button through a 'Super Intelligence' unleashed by runaway high tech!

✸✸✸

No Muska Please

A Musk Takeover

Twitter, 'the digital Town Square' according to Elon Musk, is in a churn having to swallow hard this 'big bite' by the bad boy billionaire. $44billion thumped on the Board table with such 'elan' by our new tech- baron Elon. The perfect takeover artist did it ostensibly for maintaining his image of being a 'speech absolutist' (Whatever that means). The Twitter blue bird is all of a flutter and a large chunk of Twitterati is in a blue funk.

The 'poison pill' strategy didn't work to keep Elon's marauding hands off the social media giant. It is only the likes of Socrates who can drink the cup of the poisonous hemlock to uphold their views.

Our gentle Bharat Bro, newly eased into helming Twitter, had apparently a backseat driver in the guise of Jack Dorsey who was eased out of the Twitter CEO's post under pressure. Still on the Board he has warmed up to the new maverick owner. So how could the Twitter Board refuse an enticing offer by Musk?

But the majority of the employees are not very chuffed at the modern day Croesus taking over the reins at age 50.

There are issues about no content moderation ending up in a troll invasion and less tolerance of diverse views.

Elon Musk himself displays a singular abrasiveness when criticised. And his first Tweet after twitter's privatisation in response to the alarm bells ringing around the social networking platform used by more than 200 million users every day was: 'The extreme antibody reaction from those who fear free speech says it all'!

Perfect adolescent petulance and glee at generating envy on the possession of an expensive toy. *Ab to Musk ka hai, aur Muska hi chalega!*

Who knows he may persuade Trump to get back on the platform. He tweeted his displeasure over content moderation policies of Twitter's top lawyer Vijaya Gadde straight off the bat. She was the one who barred Trump from Twitter.

Musk put his hand in his e-vehicle company Tesla Inc.'s cookie jar to scoop out some millions towards the acquisition of Twitter. He is still not spaced out with his Space X company launches giving people thrills without spills. For it was his team's innovations in making the world's first orbital class reusable rocket called Falcon 9 that has the world in thrall.

Musk's theatrics have to be taken with a big pinch of salt. Do not lose your sleep over his next takeover targets. He wants to rejig 'good ole' Coke to put cocaine back into it and even take over the friendly McDonalds to fix all the ice-cream machines. He can tweet to his heart's content with more tongue in cheek juvenile jibes since he will be the Big Boss. Elon is more a jesting knight than a jousting one.

Full marks to the Amul creative triumvirate to make instant use of the Twitter takeover in its Amul cheese advertisement. Brilliant punning with super marketing! '*Yeh cheez badi hai Musk Musk!* And the tagline, 'Share it, don't have it Elon'! is a scintillating combination of a Bollywood song, punning and soft marketing with the advice of sharing the product. Iranian cafes in Mumbai could emulate Amul and give the neighbourhood "Maska Bun' they serve an image makeover. Call it 'Musk-ka-Bun' till the current hubbub about Twitter lasts.

But then Iranian cafes in Mumbai have survived and retained their quaint character without Musk's help so far. Brittania Company has the salted biscuits advertised as '50-50: Maska Chaska'. Now the Twitterati will have to display 'Musk-ka-Chaska' willy nilly—not 50-50 but 100 percent Musk's own.

P.S. With the current imbroglio over the Twitter take over, one can only wait with bated breath to see the denouement!

***

Twitter Tantrums

Bluebird Blues

Elon Musk, the freshly minted Chief Twit of the microblogging site, holding a kitchen sink makes a perfect visual for his maiden appearance at the Twitter HQ at San Francisco. It is almost like a sneak preview of his intentions of throwing the kitchen sink at half the employees, mainly the key members of the erstwhile Twitter kitchen cabinet, who dared to take him on when he withdrew his bid of the $44 billion deal earlier. They slapped a law suit and threw the rule book at him in return. He had to eat crow and close the deal.

Musk, despite the heavyweight companies, SpaceX and Tesla, that he helms and his brilliant and futuristic entrepreneurial mind, continues to show signs of juvenile petulance and a quirky humour that borders on abrasive. The Twitter deal was handled in a 'drama queen' style which is his usual public posturing — a cocky cocktail of suspense, wacky humour and braggadocio laced with threats.

Heads rolled and a mass exodus ensued as Elon Reeve Musk a lá Donald Trump kept up the chant of 'You are fired!'. He emailed an ultimatum to the Twitter employees asking them to commit to "working long hours at high intensity" or leave. Most preferred to leave. He had to shut down the Twitter office as the staff exited en masse.

The new work ethic of 'hard core vision' entailed the expunging of the hybrid model necessitated by the Covid-19 lockdowns. No WFH (work from home), the Big Boss said, perhaps muttering sotto voce an expletive with a slightly different abbreviation. But he had to water down this diktat soon enough, with some conditions, to at least retain a skeletal staff to run the key systems.

From the kitchen sink to the linen closet, Musk advanced in his housecleaning project at the Blue Bird Headquarters in San Fran. He tweeted with a video clip displaying a closet full of '#Stay Woke' t-shirts showing covert disapproval in tone and in his thread of tweets. '#Stay woke' gained traction after the #Black Lives Matter campaign.

Elon's new 'merch' (merchandise) was T's with the slogan #Stay@work. Musk's conservative leanings are sticking out a mile from his re-instatement of those who were barred from Twitter.

Ironically, the Twitter addict Trump declined to rejoin since he has his own alt-tech social media platform, Truth Social. With his followers like QAnon, a conspiracy theorist, who was convicted for taking part in the recent attack by white supremacists on the Capitol in the U.S., one wonders at the percentage of truth in the website.

Twitter, founded by Jack Dorsey in 2016, has been around for a while with 217million monetisable users around the globe. That is massive!

To write an epitaph for a pulsating platform would be a pity.

#RIP Twitter trending now, generated by those who are leaving and trolls, might be premature. Elon Musk likes to have the last word. This time the riposte with the tweet, "Twitter is Alive" or "Maybe we've gone to heaven/hell& don't know it" is passably funny!!

✸✸✸

Tokri Tales

Weavers' Magic

It is a digital world totally in thrall of Big Tech. With gadgetry hitting the market place with ever evolving newfeatures, the dazzling array of devices strutting on world stage has truly left us to our devices. The star performers like iPhones, iPads, iPods, Smart laptops and other mind boggling gizmos rule the market place.

What chance does a humble *Tokri* with no high tech pretensions stand in this glitzy gallery, you may ask? But if one ponders for a while, pulling oneself out of the vortex of consumerism, the answer takes shape and rises to smite our conscience. Are we consumers or being consumed by greed? We are going down a slippery slope towards an environmental disaster and an eventual extinction of the humans and other species on planet Earth. The fossil records show five mass extinctions in geological time. With our natural ecosystem degraded by human greed, this realisation is dawning slowly on perceptive people who are lobbying worldwide to halt this descent.

The Gen Next is rightfully livid at the environmental degradation brought about by the old generation, hence the excoriation by Greta Thunberg, a 16 year old climate activist who chastised the assembled World leaders at the

U.N. Climate Action Summit in 2019 for stealing the dreams of the young. 'How dare You!' was her stinging rebuke. The current rate of extinction is between 100 and 1,000 times higher than the pre-human background rate of extinction. An extinction of 'Humano -Saurus' is not such a remote possibility!

The unassuming *Tokri* in a linked -in way can lead to a sustainable lifestyle in baby steps first, till the acceptance of limiting our carbon footprint catches on. This rural indigenous receptacle literally carries the load of millennia of culture, agriculture, artisanal skill, earnest livelihoods and a sense of design that should place it on the top of the podium.

Tokris of myriad shapes, sizes and material are a feast for the eyes. Each region of the world draws upon its indigenous natural materials to weave and create a piece of unique beauty. Willow and walnut wood in Kashmir, bamboo in the Northeast, banana and coconut fibre in the South, to name a few, give us a bonanza of baskets in India.

Artisanal basketry from other countries takes shape in the form of fancy rattan baskets from Indonesia, reed grass ones from Bali, and many tribal people use cedar bark, swamp grass and whatever pliable material locally available.

I am a 'basket case for *Tokris* and have a motley collection from my travels. They always bring a smile to my lips and a prayer too that may these unsung craftspeople be rewarded and blessed.

***

Daily Ragas: Rhythm of Life

TAIL
PIECES
The News

Daily Raga

Variegated Rhythms of Daily Life

The patch of sky framed by the window begins to take on a lighter hue. Bunches of sun-yellow flowers and brown pendulous pods festoon every branch of the glorious *Amaltas*, truly called the Golden Shower tree, that spreads jauntily outside my window. It is daybreak. The morning silence has a soothing touch. With a thud the rubber-banded roll of newspapers lands like a guided missile at our doorstep. With that it is time for the neighbourhood medley to begin.

Clanging vessels and tinkling cups herald the making of the brew that cheers. Pressure cookers hiss as freshly made food is readied for the tiffins. *Chapatis* being made on the hot *tawa* send a familiar aroma wafting up. Car engines rev up in the parking lot below as people set off for work. Scooters are kick –started, purr to life and go off on their journey with a hoarse hoot. Macho bikes roar down the street to their destinations. Cycle rickshawallahs with their matchbox-sized seating contraptions trill their bells summoning the little ones to their nursery schools. School-goers bursting with energy go bounding down the steps in their crisp uniforms. Loud and peppy music, combined with exhortations to shake a leg, emanate from an aerobic class being conducted in the house below. Thus is played the 'Morning Raga' everyday.

After a brief interlude begins another movement in this daily raga with the arrival of the vendors, who seek the attention of the households in their distinctive style. Their cries punctuate the hours with their singsong signature renditions. The *sabziwalla* with his stentorian voice chants a rapid-fire inventory of his greens as he pushes the cycle cart down the road. Many windows are flung open and window-shopping carried to its literal conclusion. Next are the syncopated cries of the *raddiwalla.* He diligently plies his trade, unaware that recycling is the buzzword these days. As if to reinforce the recycling ethic comes the *bartanwali* with a high-pitched soprano cry. She entices housewives into exchanging old clothes for utensils. It is a bargain few can resist.

Occasionally an old generator splutters to life striking a jarring note. A recurring motif in this medley is the clanging sound on an iron griddle orchestrated by the *dosawalla*, who churns out hot dosas. The afternoon sonata is played on a languorous note. A melange of sounds comes forth from various households. There is the crackle of dramatic sound byte from TV buffs addicted to their daily dose of movies. Lilting Indi-pop is heard from some quarters whereas some wallow in nostalgia listening to 'oldie-goldies', melodious songs from the fifites. All these sounds form a familiar backdrop to the day's activities.

The evening brings the medley full-circle. Snatches from the morning raga are played in an 'allegro' mode now that the day's hurly-burly is done. As the light begins to fade, children return from the park chasing each other with whoops of delight. Old folks walk along at an unhurried pace. Robert Browning's lines, "God is in Heaven and all's right with the world," come to my mind. Somewhere in the distance a dog barks with an authoritative growl. Thus goes the circadian rhythm of life. And with nightfall it is time to surrender oneself to the sounds of silence again.

Who says there is no poetry in the quotidian?

Jollygood Bollywood

Our Ambassadors at Large

The place was Surin— a small town in Thailand. The event—an elephant round up that enacts the Burmese invasion on Thai soil and how it was repelled. The year was 1987 and to witness this recreation of a piece of history were gathered, amongst others, diplomats from all over the world. Amidst all the fanfare and trumpeting, a familiar song crackled over the loud speakers. Did I hear it right? I did a double take when I looked over my shoulder. "*Chal Chal Chal Mere Haathi*" was being played to keep time with the prancing steps of a pachyderm!

It struck me then with force that it is not just us 'desis' who are smitten by the glitzy stardust of Bollywood. The 'masala movies' have made inroads into the hearts of people in many parts of the world. It was Hindi films again that created a fleeting bond with a total stranger in an alien land while touring with the military attaché corps in Surat Thani, a southern Thai town. We were riding in a local variant of the cycle rickshaw. On seeing a sari-clad lady, a little urchin swung his hips in imitation of Bollywood heroines and kept on chanting, Hema Malini in a sing song manner. The dream girl had crossed the shores of India into the interiors of this distant city.

From *"Alam Aara"* to *"K3G"* the canvas of the Hindi films is mind boggling. There are different strokes for different folks. From frothy romance, historical extravaganza, patriotic fervour, family drama to mythological melodrama — you name the flavour and they have it. The Bollywood script writers steer a story through labyrinthine twists and turns, toss a full quota of '*dishum dishum*' choreographed with telling effect, dish up dollops of sentimentality, churn a melange of comedy and tear-jerker situations, seasoned with a dash of oomph. The emotional catharsis for the viewer is so complete that one feels cleansed.

Some people are toffee-nosed about the song and dance routine with heaving bosom and swaying hips. But the dream merchants know the pulse of the masses. These films are a passport to a magical world, transporting one from harsh and crushing reality to a euphoric Utopia — however short lived. Where can you get a product that gives you such a large slice of life, all for the price of an affordable ticket?

Let alone the masses, even Hollywood is knocking at the our doorstep. What with the movie "Moulin Rouge" not only being in Bollywood format, but actually uses the song "chamma chamma"! So it is about time to drop the snooty chip from the shoulder as well as the disdainful sobriquet "Follywood" for Mumbai films.

I would call Bollywood and the film stars unacknowledged ambassadors of India. Way back in the fifties, Raj Kapoor was as much of an icon as Nehru in the erstwhile Soviet Union. In war-torn Afghanistan, Hindi films have begun shoring up the existing fund of goodwill for Indians. Pakistanis too enjoy the masala movies immensely. It is perhaps good strategy to use '*reelpolitik*' instead of 'realpolitik' to build bridges with other countries. Such is the credibility of Hindi films now that the movie "*Lagaan*" is analysed by corporates to glean lessons in man-management, building team spirit and motivation. All one can say is *Bollywood Tujhe Salaam!*

Kitchen Cabinet Flavours

A Melting Pot of Memories

My kitchen tells a tale! But to tweak the Bard a little—it is a tale full of sound and fury signifying something. The recipe books lining one shelf are much thumbed and dog-eared. I see guest lists and menus for the numerous parties tucked amidst the pages for the last two decades.

Such an archival culinary record evokes nostalgia for the fun-filled evenings spent with friends at various Air Force Stations. Names indicating the provenance of the dish, in meticulously written recipes, take me down memory lane. The bouquet of recipes given by various friends to beef up my limited culinary repertoire, stare back from the pages and I am caught in 'rewind' euphoria. There is Guddi's Chicken Paprika— almost *cordon bleu* standard, Havovi's nifty Ras-Malai, Neena's scrumptious Kaju Chicken and many more.

Like the aroma books for children, I can smell the whiff of Rogan Josh on the recipe page with tell-tale red gravy smudges. It is a great recap of how from faltering steps in the kitchen one evolved over time into an acceptable cook—of course with tips and guidance given with readiness and affection from more experienced Services wives—an abiding trait in the Services ethos.

The pots and pans in my 'kitchen cabinet' narrate a story of their own. The sturdy wok, with layers of carbon deposited on its bottom, is redolent of the many good meals cooked in it. The steel kettle on the tray, having steeled itself against the daily knocks of life in the kitchen, presents a bruised and dented image. But each cup of tea poured from it pours out a collage of the past. Only if I knew the art of reading tea leaves in a cup, I could predict the future too! The toaster may not be the toast of the town but it has 'attitude.' The lever refuses to get depressed unless you bully it with a heavy hand. And the mighty pressure cooker having lived a life under pressure is beginning to show signs of crankiness. It lets off steam by hissing menacingly and occasionally spews its liquid in a defiant show of wilfulness!

And looking at the *mise-en-scene* sitting atop the kitchen hob is the brass Samovar my mother gave me. It churns up nostalgia about my childhood and youth in Kashmir. The cinnamon-laden aroma of hot 'kahwa' is a delicious memory that refuses to fade out.

✸✸✸

Know Your Onions

How about 'Mutton No Pyaza'?

Alas! It is a tearjerker all right. This Asiatic herb, with its pungent edible bulb imparts the right zing to many an Indian curry. Or it used to till the prices kept zooming northwards and this earthy vegetable has an unearthly price tag attached to it now. The spectacle of the world's third largest supplier of onions reduced to tears without onions is an intriguing sight indeed. This lavender coloured orb has climbed back into the news and it is streets ahead of other vegetables. It no longer goes hand in hand with its root buddy—the wholesome potato. Even the tomatoes are blushing at being downgraded in the pecking order of prices.

An onion may be meant to lurk discreetly in gravies but it has aggressively plonked itself on centre stage. Not too long ago this subterranean denizen had grabbed the prime slots in the media and was the stuff of ministerial parleys and declarations —not to speak of hotfoot-international trade diplomacy. A plane-load of this pungent stuff had to be airlifted from neighbouring nations to soften the blow and thicken the gravy. The sting in the tail is that the taxpayer has to bear the burden of the import. So there'll be tears either way, with onions or without. To ease the squeeze and churn out curries without worries, the government has to slap a ban on the export of this rapscallion from time to time. This helps in tiding over the temporary shortages of the onions and to also mend the short fuses of the avid consumers.

Resolving this all-pervasive onion crisis becomes top political priority every once in a while. In this highly charged atmosphere, time is ripe for the "State of the Onion" speeches. There is just no knowing where this Old Faithful—or rather the lack of this Old Faithful—will lead us.

Perhaps we don't need to be so teary-eyed about this perennial onion saga. There is a lesson crying out to be learnt here. We have to use consumer resistance as a weapon in times of scarcity. Only then will the hoarders and middlemen be prevented from making a kill. Now is the time to try some of our most delectable dishes in which onions play a secondary role or no role at all.

So the time has come to get to know your cookery onions and switch from 'Mutton Do Pyaza' to 'Mutton No Pyaza'! A small sacrifice indeed to make, to be free from the stranglehold of this tiny orb.

***

Mirror, Mirror on the Wall

Vanity Mirrored

I see it fully borne out everyday. In fact, each time the door- bell rings. The myth of Narcissus is alive and well amidst us. It is re-enacted in a slightly modified form at our door- step. No ponds at the threshold in which to gaze admiringly at one's reflection. What I do have is a round mirror with a wrought iron frame, on the wall at the entrance to our house. It is there simply because of its inability to find a niche inside the flat. Unwittingly it has proved to be an amazing tool in giving me an insight into human psychology.

I see these acts of self-adoration through our wire-mesh front door. A gaggle of delivery folks, my daily domestic help and other sundry visitors form the subjects of my study. All seem to have a fatal attraction for the mercury-coated piece of glass on the wall. The Narcissist's Gallery has some interesting portraits indeed. Arjun, the teenage 'chokra' from the neighbourhood grocery store presses the bell and is in no hurry to see me appear at the door. He stares fixedly at his image, oblivious of my arrival, occasionally humming a catchy film-song. It is his way of introducing some fantasy in his otherwise drab routine of delivering stuff. Shashi, the sweepress, always dressed to kill, may forget to wield the broom on the staircase but never fails to steal a glance at the mirror. 'Vanity thy name is woman', as the Bard said, so why blame her. Mahesh, the '*presswalla*', while waiting to collect his bundle of clothes for ironing, beguiles himself by assessing his image in the mirror from every angle. Manjula, our maid, who generally completes her chores with lightning speed, has always a moment to spare as she checks out the visage she presents to the world. The gas deliveryman, who announces his arrival with a thunderous roll of the cylinder from a mile off, also falls an easy prey to the seductive charm of the siren on the wall.

The tally of victims continues to swell each day. The other day I caught, Munne Lal, our staid looking post- man, in the act of mopping his brow in front of the mirror. He had a sheepish look as if to say that such vanity was avoidable. At last count I had the '*raddiwalla*' also on the muster roll of the self-absorbed. Irfaan, the pint- sized boy from the meat shop, not even ten as yet, finds it difficult to peek into the mirror because of his lack of height. This doesn't deter him from pushing a '*gamla*' against the wall and use it as a stepping stone to reach the magic mirror in order to admire his visage unabashedly. One curious vignette that intrigues me still was the courier delivery boy greeting his reflection in the mirror Maori style, nose to nose! Now each time the doorbell rings I hang back deliberately to see if the magic mirror will cast its spell or not.

Not all mortals are given to a vainglorious use of the mirror. Shah Jahan, the mighty Mughal, not an ordinary mortal by any yardstick, used the mirror to assuage a sentimental ache. Imprisoned by his son Aurangzeb at

Agra Fort, he was able to lessen the blow of bitter captivity by gazing upon the reflection of Taj Mahal in a mirror. However, the mirror on my wall has served its own humble purpose. It has certainly proved the worthy poet wrong, who said, 'What's this life, if full of care, We have no time to stand and stare'!

Hair! Hair!

Hair Raising Styles

Myth, legend and folklore are awash with a sea of stories about the crowning glory of Gods, Goddesses and mere mortals. Lord Shiva, so the story goes, with his divine powers trapped River Ganga in his matted locks and released it slowly in seven streams to prevent a deluge on earth. The secret of the Biblical hero, Samson's super human strength lay in his hair. Ensnared in the honey trap set by the deadly Delilah, he was shorn of his hair while asleep, thus losing his might and machismo with a snip of the scissors.

Think of long tresses and one pin-up that pops up inevitably is that of Lady Godiva. A medieval noblewoman who went riding on a horse through the town of Coventry "clad in naught but tresses" and one forgets that she did this full monty not for naked exhibitionism. Interestingly enough, this dramatic solo- tableau was enacted as a mark of protest against the oppressive taxes imposed on the general populace. Here was an activist eons ahead of her time!

Most of us brought up on a diet of Grimm's fairy tales know the rhyme "Rapunzel, Rapunzel, let down your hair". She of the golden hair cascaded them down the castle window to pull up the enchantress by day and 'rope in' her Prince Charming at night. A darker myth tells the tale of

Gorgon Medusa, one of a trio of sisters, with her snake-haired dreadlocks, who could 'petrify' one with her fierce gaze. Closer home, our Indian Goddesses are shown in calendar art a la Ravi Varma, with luxuriant well groomed hair. It is only in their 'aggro' avatar that their hair is dishevelled and wild.

The Hippies in the sixties with their bohemian life-style defiantly sported long hair as an 'in-your-face' rebellious stance against a staid society. The iconic Broadway rock-musical "Hair" had an amazing run singing paeans to free love and long tresses. Bollywood and cricket, with their high glamour quotient have always set the hearts of their followers aflutter. We had our own Audrey Hepburn in Sadhana of yesteryears with her fringe called the 'Sadhana cut' and the evergreen actor Dev Anand with his Gregory Peck puff romancing his leading ladies. Some of our cricketing icons have had bold manes. Let alone domestic fans, even the mercurial General Musharraf from across the border couldn't resist commenting approvingly on Dhoni's long hair. A novel tribute to Sachin's hundredth hundred was paid by a Delhi salon— a Sachin hair-style for just hundred bucks. Aamir Khan used an innovative promotional gimmick for his movie, *Ghajini.* Trimming the tuft on his head to carve out the title of the movie was an act in turn cloned by his die-hard cine-fans all over India. A clever strategy that for a free and eye-catching advertising space!

From bouffant to bob, from chignon to grunge, Afro to braided hair tribal-style, hair-styles follow the dictates of fickle fashion. Despite the heft gained by 'men without manes' banding together as the Baldies International, wig-makers, trichologists, hair-stylists and the hair-care industry are laughing all the way to the bank.

But crass-commerce apart, in the revered Tirupati temple, the devotees follow a centuries old tradition of making offerings of tonsured hair to Lord Venkateswara —a symbolic shedding of vanity. Mind-boggling stats show a thousand kilos of hair shorn and offered every day. This rich harvest of hair is e-auctioned through global tenders and enriches the temple coffers.

The Chinese, amongst others, are the most avid buyers of Indian hair for their wig-making industry. This is one hirsute 'growth story' where India has pipped China to the post, or the 'pate', should we say, in the on-going China-India competition in Asia.

Well, it may be hair today and gone tomorrow but there is no ignoring this crop on the head. To this, a resounding Hair! Hair!

✸✸✸

Maid For Each Other

Memsaab' and 'Ayah Log' Made for Each Other

The sheer prowess of maids achieved by fair means or foul, has been the stuff of breaking news recently. A maid in Manhattan, unlike the story- line in the Jennifer Lopez movie bearing the same name, made headlines some years ago by being involved in an unpleasant episode with a celebrity gent. The scandal cost the man his job and ruined his chances of attaining the highest post as the head of a European nation.

Closer home a maid muddied the reputation of a Bollywood actor nipping his star career in the bud. But it was a maid yet again whose daring rescue of the little boy Moshe at the Chabad House during 26/11 terror attack, at great peril to her life, tugged at the heart – strings of one and all.

From the conniving to the noble one has seen maids of all stripes and shades. You love them or hate them, but the maid dependency in a certain class of society remains undiminished. No wonder the maid-agencies are raking in the moolah hands on fist.

Having led a nomadic existence as an armed forces wife, handling the elusive phenomenon called the 'Ayah' ('aya' seldom, gone often) has been quite an experience. In my salad days as a housewife, with my abysmal cooking abilities, the maid seemed to me a saviour of damsels in distress. With the armed forces culture of party-time at the drop of a hat one always placed a well-trained maid on a high pedestal. If the said domestic happened to be AWOL (absent without official leave), the entire household was in disarray.

But Alas! that breed of maids is fast vanishing. The ones that are around call the shots. In fact maids impose their own set of coditionalities a la IMF before they agree to don the mantle of the Abigail in your household.

A sophisticated rating system that could well match Moody's, the credit rating agency, has been devised by the maids (no less moody!) to assess the 'memsaab log'. The star billing in their list of prospective employers is given to newly married couples, who in their euphoric state would think nothing of stockpiles of sugar and other provisions dwindling in record time. A young couple with one child is tolerable according to their Q.R's for choosing a household. If you have two kids or more, a frown will certainly crease the ayah's brow at the additional work. Your approval ratings will take a nosedive if you happen to have a combo of two kids, aged parents and a dog to boot.

These uppity 'ayah log' are generally a metro phenomenon. Some of our far- flung military stations still have a dwindling breed of good khansamas and ayahs. The smarter metro- maids, with higher aspirations and a facility in spoken English look out for armed forces families going on diplomatic assignments abroad. No 'desi saab' will do for them. Well, grant it to them, we all want to improve our job prospects. If we have the 'yuppies', why not the upwardly mobile ayahs? A vacuum-cleaner, a rice-cooker, a micro-wave oven, a washing machine are a must to make you earn their respect. Broader and fancier the range of gadgets that you possess, the higher you are on their totem-pole of employers.

The attitude the maids wear on their shoulders, like epaulettes on a uniform, does rile one often. At times one is tempted to throw off the shackles of 'maid-dom' by turning to the new fuzzy- logic machines and other household gizmos. But remember that one long spell of power-shedding will send you scurrying back into the arms of the 'fuzzier- logic' ayahs.

So all said and done, this luxury of a human gadget in the avatar of an ayah is most welcome. Take it from me; don't be too finicky, as a 'maid to order' is a tall order indeed!

✸✸✸

Ring and Bring

Deliverance at the Door

Metro lifestyle has a frenetic pace all its own. It leaves you, more often than not, with your tongue lolling out. What with the nuclear family and the double income group being the norm, time is always at a premium. Despite the fancy tags of Super-Mom and Super-Dad for the high-flying mod couple, managing the whole caboodle of home, office and the market place puts one in a real orbit.

The era of dependable domestic help is a fading memory. If you're not lucky enough to possess a general dogsbody to run errands for you, the chances of your frothing at the mouth are very bright indeed.

This is where 'deliverance' comes in the form of a home-delivery system. A perfect niche for entrepreneurs of all kinds. Everything is a phone call away—from *swadeshi* to *videshi* brands in groceries, aerated drinks, ice creams and most of all fast foods. The Great Indian Middle Class that is being eyed so covetously by many trading nations, is itself engaged in eyeing greedily the gustatory delights offered by the home-delivery operators.

The food scene particularly has the competition hotting up. You don't have to dream about 'Tandoori Nights' or

'Bhaji on the Beach' anymore! It is all here — a tinkle away and delivered at your doorstep. The leaflets stuck in your mailbox or slipped under the door offer you a bouquet of seductive cuisine in enticing text. One leaflet not given to poetic flourishes had this terse command in bold red letters—YOU RING, WE BRING! Doggerel verse notwithstanding, when I ordered some macaroons what was delivered was macaroni! Another enterprise in our neighbourhood had a person, not too conversant with the English tongue, taking phone orders. When I asked him if he stocked a particular brand of cereal, he chuckled and told me to tune into Door- Darshan for whatever 'serials' I wanted! So one has to concede that home -delivery has its own pitfalls at times.

But the business savvy entrepreneurs are totally in sync with the new generation. With pagers and mobile phones attended by dulcet voiced lasses, they are a perfect example of good PR. A few far-sighted ones, aware of the windfalls of the information highway, have gone high-tech and set up websites for home delivery.

Not so fancy, but still I am amazed at the bonanza of home-delivery service in our neighbourhood. The drycleaner has a pick-up van and home delivery service, the butcher delivers the choicest cuts through a pert looking *'chotu'*, the *Halwai* has piping hot *jalebis* sent in a melting moment. The chemist has the medicines delivered in promptly at your doorstep. If you happen to be sick, with no 'gofers' around, this is an act of mercy.

Not a phone-order delivery but through word of mouth, even a *'maalish-waali'* turns up at the doorstep. And some of them are now sporting the cell phone to spread the message and the massage!

Apart from the tangible advantage of home delivery, I discovered some fringe benefits too. An enterprising take-away food joint had printed this curious flyer, which could be a copywriter's inspiration. It listed tariff for its homely *thaali* meals, of Standard, Deluxe and Executive variety, apart from other exotica. They promised to give you a discount if you ordered on a 'monthali' basis. Superior punning or inferior spellings—it's anybody's guess!

✱✱✱

Chai-Paani

Baksheesh Indian Style

The world is a global village now with instant connectivity thanks to the telecom revolution. With a constant buzz on social networking sites like Facebook, YouTube, Twitter and many more, we are all LinkedIn. It wasn't so a few decades ago, with satellite television not having spread its tentacles around the globe to usher in the monotony of cultural uniformity. In the sixties countries other than one's own did have a certain mystique about them. Travel abroad was not so common and the lucky few who went on such jaunts were the objects of great envy. Not being *au fait* with another culture could sometimes cause a hiccup or two. This was fully borne out in one such cultural interface in which I was a minor *dramatis personae*. But let me begin at the beginning. I am sure all of us have a nugget stored in our memory bank about some occasion in our lives when we were left tongue-tied. Of course, the possibilities of smart rejoinders always seem endless after the event. But therein lies the rub!

On a cool winter morning in Delhi, while standing at the gate of a South Delhi house, I happened to be in the company of two dapper armed forces officers. One was my aviator husband and the other my brother-in-law, a "pucca" infantry colonel of the Indian Army. A car with a CD number plate caught our attention as it slowed down in front of us. A gaggle of heads stuck out from every window. They were scanning the house numbers with fierce concentration. The family obviously from alien shores was new to our land. They drove off only to return to the same spot again in a trice. But now they had bewilderment writ large on their faces. One didn't need face reading skills to see that they were playing the "house – hunting" game in which our countrymen display considerable prowess. Indians think it is their karma to be lost in housing colonies. The sign posting in many residential areas in our land seems to be the handiwork of a budding misanthrope! Not only does the numbering follow a whimsical order, but many a time the arrow points sky-wards. A symbolic indication that God alone can help you now!

Little did these unsuspecting foreign souls know that to decipher any logic in the numbering of the houses would need the acumen of a mathematician of the calibre of Ramanujan and the patience of Job. Seeing them in such dire distress, an offer of navigational assistance made to the hapless family by my husband and brother -in-law was eagerly accepted. Thus the combined might of the Air-Force and the Army was deployed to conduct "Operation Track-down".

The paterfamilias at the wheel off-loaded a couple of his progeny to take the volunteer guides on board to accomplish the mission. Shortly afterwards they returned, this time looking very triumphant. Ostensibly they had cracked the jig-saw puzzle. The Good Samaritans got down smartly from the car, happy at having conducted this minor rescue mission with lightning speed.

The armed forces officers are trained to handle all crises with total cool and display remarkable finesse and aplomb in handling any untoward situation both in war and peace. What happened next was certainly one such situation. To express his gratitude for the trouble taken to render this assistance to him, the foreign gent dipped into his wallet and pulled out some crisp notes saying cheerily, "Here is for Chai".

For once I saw these fine armed forces specimens totally speechless, but only for a split second. They smiled benignly at the foreigner and walked away. Some over-zealous foreign office staffer had apparently briefed this emissary too well on 'Baksheesh' Indian style!

Air Warriors

Puny Adversary vs the Macho Air-Warrior

Having been the better half of an air warrior husband for more than forty years, one has seen the sterling qualities of these macho men with their magnificent flying machines up close and personal. Nothing fazes these guys. Well, so I thought till my retired air warrior husband was felled by the puny dengue mosquito recently. The back-breaking Dengue confined him to bed for more than two weeks. He kept cribbing that the only other time he had been forced to lie in bed for so long was when as a twenty year old aviator he was involved in the crash- landing of a Dakota aircraft, on a flight from Kargil, on the boulder strewn Rambiara riverbed close to Srinagar in the Kashmir valley. He survived to tell the tale!

However, this winged Dengue adversary has declared open season for deadly attacks on warriors and non-warriors alike. Alarming reports of dengue fever causing almost a meltdown of the platelet count and worse are the talk of the town. What puzzles me immensely is that in this day and age when mankind (Do we need to rephrase that word?) has developed an arsenal of lethal weapons to destroy the world twice-over, it hasn't come up with a fool-proof device to combat a puny aerial menace. Despite the combat between man and mosquito being unequal, the pesky creature continues to thrive and unleash deadly diseases.

This dengue causing mosquito goes by the imposing name of *Aedes egypti* and it is the female bite that is responsible for the spread of dengue and a smorgasbord of other illnesses like chikungunya and yellow fever! *Anopheles,* the genus name of Greek origin, for the malarial variety, imparts a certain euphonious distinction to this fly-by-night operator. To the literary minded it probably evokes a sound association with the Greek writer Aristophanes, whose biting satire is matched by the biting prowess of this mosquito.

These mosquitoes seem to have adopted techniques of warfare against humans as if they have been to a war-gaming school. Guerrilla warfare is their trump card. They launch nocturnal or day sorties from hidden bases. With the precision of a heat-seeking missile they zero-in on the target and bite and scoot doing a VTOL (vertical take- off and landing) At times we get an advance warning of sorts with the buzzing in our ears, but we can only flail about in anger and frustration at this nano-sized adversary. We almost need to deploy an air borne warning and control system (AWACS) to shield ourselves.

The Bard in his poetic exuberance could write about "A Midsummer Night's Dream" but then he didn't have to contend with squadrons of aerial invaders in season and out of season. It is not surprising that a light dive bomber of World War 11 vintage was christened "Mosquito"— a grudging acknowledgement of the might of this aerial enemy.

Underestimating and dismissing the enemy as a negligible threat, a mosquito net was considered enough of a deterrent for the pest earlier. But over the years, this menace has spawned a whole industry of mosquito repellents in creams and coils to protect us from the cussed 'night-errant'—the devious enemy that subjects you to an involuntary blood donation.

Whether it is an apocryphal story or not, it is said that Indian history would have taken a different turn but for the puny mosquito. When Alexander the Great, in his triumphant march across the plains of Punjab, kept advancing across the River Jhelum and the Indus, at some point his soldiers refused to go any further. The reason was not battle fatigue but the persistent mosquito menace that left the soldiers in an enfeebled state. It is a humbling thought that makes one reluctantly admit that in the ultimate analysis, to borrow a phrase from Bollywood—*"Jo Jeeta Wohi Sikander!"*

Home Safari!

Thrills and Chills

'Staycation' is a well-tossed word with a subtext of sour grapes perhaps. I have a similar word to launch in word-space—'Home Safari'. No big cats here sauntering past your van in exotic locales. This home safari has all the thrills and chills served up close and personal without burning a hole in your pocket. What's more you have a ring-side view.

The world is awash with green activists. Rightly so. Greening the environment is their rallying cry— Trump's tantrums notwithstanding. 'Live and let Live' is a clarion call reverberating around Planet Earth. I, an ordinary denizen of this glorious Gaia, with a tiny carbon footprint am surrounded by an assortment of God's creatures. No I don't live in a tree-house. I am a city dweller in an area not totally bereft of trees.

PETA please don't get me wrong but my day begins with a rant against the ants. I am told they never sleep! I quite believe it. Their 'antenna' is always up. Awesome in their intelligence gathering and brilliant in logistics, the ants are a lesson in industriousness. The tiniest of food particles is sighted and carted away in the blink of an eye. An Ant-Fed Express of sorts delivering to the ant silos. The route march of ants of varied hues, sizes and bites continues uninterrupted. Do what you will, they are in cruise control.

Next set of actors in this home safari are the cooing pigeons in pairs. They stake their claim to every window ledge and perch around the house. The resident pigeons are always on a recce with beady eyes to find a suitable nesting place. They sneak in when one's back is turned. When shooed off they get into a real flap. Pirouetting on fan blades, clinging to window grills and even hopping on to the bed in panic, these feathered friends anoint the floor and objects generously before finding an exit through the window. Interestingly, it was the 'pigeon-encounter' that led to Jahangir being besotted by Noorjehan's beauty and wit. Young Salim left a pair of pet pigeons in her safekeeping at a *Meena Bazaar*. She promptly released one. Angry at this transgression he demanded to know how could the pigeon fly off. She released the other one to show him how! Noorjehan went on to become the most powerful Mughal Empress. With this royal connection, one has to cut some slack for these avian intruders.

Bollywood in its cinematic paean to pigeons and the Walled City in 'Delhi 6' even composed a hit song on a pert little pigeon named Masakali.

The ant-antics and the pigeon shenanigans are minor performances in this urban safari. The real frisson is generated by the monkeys. The simians with their intelligence and agility are not so easily intimidated. They lope in through an open window and indulge in food, fun and frolic — occasionally knocking down some crystal with their free-flowing movements. It is crystal clear, they don't give a hoot.

The monkey brigade has been causing a great deal of consternation to 'Babudom' in the corridors of power in Delhi. This '*vanar-sena*' invades the offices defiling the sacrosanct files causing mayhem.

To add some spice to the home-safari come the leaping lizards. Hiding in nooks generally they race up the walls Spiderman-style with great acumen. They can even hang from the ceiling like a trapeze artist while stalking a prey at night. These encounters alert us to the crush on habitat and nudge us to go easy on greed.

Despite the niggling irritants, there is another side to this man-nature interface. I can see and hear the cuckoo calling seductively from amongst the branches of a lusciously laden mango tree, the Drongo dangling on the high-tension wires, the turmeric-yellow *Amaltas* blossoms defiantly fresh in the summer heat and the bright and bushy-tailed squirrels going up and down trees with total insouciance. The tiny brown sparrows, with their guest appearances, bring cheer with their high-pitched chirrups.

This reminds me of the exemplary empathy John Keats displayed in a letter: "If a Sparrow come before my window, I take part in its existence".

This was written two hundred years ago. We need to wake up and face some 'inconvenient truths'. Or else face extinction!

***

Vegetables Strike Back

Cool Cukes and Blushing Tomatoes

'You are such a cabbage' is no longer a snide remark! Look at the hotting *'sabzi-scene'* currently playing in front of our startled eyes. The veg-market is giving the stock market a run for its money. Vegetables are no longer vegetating, I am afraid. Unable to learn from the cool cucumber, we are frothing at the mouth at this turn of events. The runaway prices are causing untold anguish to the *aam adami*. More so to the *aam aurat*, if you ask me, who has to bear the brunt of household budgets gone awry. Our national budget, a number crunching exercise, is easier to re-jig. But the veggies with their upmarket prices have created a fiscal deficit in the domestic budget that is hard to bridge.

Time and again, these vegetable crises blow-up in our unsuspecting faces. The reasons vary. Sometimes it is the feeble monsoon, many a time a mismatch between demand and supply, and more often greed and hoarding. Whatever the reason, it's enough to cause rumblings in the corridors of power and even louder grumbling among the consumers.

Earlier we've had one or two actors from the veg-world, individually or in concert, causing a horticultural cacophony. But this time around it is a jing-bang veg-orchestra striking discordant notes. Potato, a kitchen staple, has made even the couch-potatoes sit up and take notice. Hand in hand or rather hand in glove with its root buddy, the onion, the duo of a*loo-pyaaz* has left the *aam janata* in a pool of tears. Sporadic war-cries of boycotting some veggies by tweaking recipes is not helping either. Chicken-no-pyaza instead of Chicken-do-pyaza will take you some distance only. But the onion, with its ring upon ring remains enigmatic and gives a stinging reply to these acts of rebellion.

The tomatoes are blushing with pride at being almost at the top of the totem-pole. They are losing no time in tom-tomming their social-climbing act in the vegetable-hierarchy. We can only save ourselves the blushes or turn a beet-root red by ignoring this braggadocio.

Cauliflower, overcome by the general euphoria of the green-world, has a scandalous price tag attached to it. I think it's having an identity crisis, thinking itself to be an exotic flower and not an ordinary vegetable.

One wonders if the '*haut-sabzis*' are having a fancy ramp-show to compete with *haute* couture. This is certainly their moment in the sun. Even the gnarled and ungainly ginger has to be approached gingerly because of its price. *Karela,* the bitter gourd, is living up to its name. We certainly are left with a bitter taste in the mouth.

The ever-green leafy spinach, is also beyond our grasp and we are all turning blue in the face with this green terrorism. And the tiny green chilly, often the only accompaniment to a poor person's *roti,* is also sending a chill down the spine with its pungent price. The common *bhindi* is also assuming aristocratic airs of being a Lady, and showing us the finger. Not wanting to be left in the wings, the drumsticks are beating the drum on a high decibel note to announce their arrival on centre-stage.

However this mutiny in the vegetable kingdom is giving us kitchen blues. The maestros conducting this jing -bang orchestra are partly the middlemen and traders out to make a fast buck. The *Sarkar* says it is taking urgent steps to tame the volatile prices for bringing in *achhe din* with an export ban on the *aam aloo.* More *Kisaan Mandis* for direct selling, cold storage chains and new technology to avoid waste have been promised.

But in the meantime, we are waiting with bated breath and empty baskets. If this does not happen pronto, I am afraid, life will be a lemon!

✷✷✷

And Quiet Flows the Ganga

Eternal Cycle of Life and Death

In the sweltering heat of summer even at 6 a.m. the family set off to the nearest crematorium, appropriately called, *Antim Niwas*—the final address— to collect the mortal remains of my brother-in-law. A handful of bones and ashes is all that remained of a healthy army man felled by the emperor of maladies — the invidious cancer that steals upon a body to conduct a secret warfare to attack it and render it lifeless.

As a rite of passage to the other world, Shantanu, the young Pujari, consecrated the Asthi with chanting of mantras. The ashes were collected with an admixture of rose petals, dry fruit and milk and placed in an earthen pot. His daughter and only child Anjali, was here from London to offer her Shraddhanjali to her beloved father.

The millennial connection with the holy Ganga persists uninterrupted in our cultural and religious traditions. The immersion of ashes in the waters of River Ganges is symbolic of merging with this life-giving force. Ganga Ma, revered as a Mother, takes the body back into her lap cleansing it of all its sins.

This final submersion in water also brings full-circle the five elements that form our bodies. The body is consigned to the flames on the earth, when your breath becomes air, immersed in the waters of the holy river and it goes on to become part of the ether.

True to this tradition we set off in a car to the nearest spot from our area where Ganga flows, though in reduced majesty. Garh Ganga in Uttar Pradesh is a bustling town, about 150 kilometres from Noida, with a well organised and bustling death-industry.

There seems to be fierce competition amongst the service providers to claim the ashes. Just short of reaching the place, you find you are being tailed by young bike riding boys who want to hustle you into their motorised boat for the last ride for the deceased. Before the immersion yet another priest negotiates the charges to do a mini-puja.

Clutching the earthen pot with the ashes we sit in the boat and go to the middle of the river. Finally there is a sense of calm and the contents are poured in and the clay pot is also lowered into the bosom of the holy river. Each of us confronts this personal encounter with mortality with a huge sense of loss.

Before going back another ritual of feeding the hungry on the Ghat is to be completed. In no time you have a gaggle of urchins, old women, men and sadhus materialise in front of the Halwai shop. Each one is given piping hot puris topped with two laddoos. The urchins have fisticuffs grabbing the food and the money given as dakshina and still follow you to the car demanding more! Some of those being fed surreptitiously throw the puris into the garbage. Since there is a constant flow of people coming to the Ghat, this is no surprise.

Since life and death walk hand in hand, the National Highway is studded with food points. Shiva Dhaba is the preferred name since Lord Shiva caught the Ganges in his tresses. Having satiated the soul of the departed, the families stop at the highway dhabas to satiate their own hunger. And quietly flows the Ganga seeing this eternal cycle of life and death!

Hullabaloo in the Mango Orchard

Mango Mania

This is most certainly not meant as a disrespectful riff on the famed author Kiran Desai's acclaimed debut novel- 'Hullabaloo in the Guava Orchard' which fictionalises an intriguingly true story of a man who lives on a guava tree for fifteen years and ends up being taken for a holy man. There are no such twists in my account of the mango tree. Not an orchard really but a neighbour's garden with this towering mango tree. And I am not a fit candidate to live in a tree house.

But *Mangifera indica,* to give mango its botanical name, is inextricably woven into the cultural texture of India dating back more than 4,000 years. The sea-faring Portuguese on their arrival in Kerala were fascinated by this fruit and put it on the global stage. It was the Portuguese general Afonso de Albuquerque who lent his name to Alfonso, the king of fruits. The Mughals despite their internecine strife were united in their love for mangoes. And how can can we forget the obsessive love for mangoes that the famous Urdu poet Mirza Ghalib had. So my admiration for the mango tree in my neighbourhood is part of my cultural psyche.

It is a towering mango tree with straying branches that always gets a second look from passers by. A tall mango-picker rests tantalisingly against the main trunk.

I could see this thickly leaf-clad tall tree across our cluster from our kitchen window during the lockdown. What a blessing it was, for it kept greening my thoughts while I grappled with the reality of dirty dishes in the sink. From the time the Mango flowers appeared on the second big fork of the trunk turning into green mangoes (almost camouflaged in the greenery) I was almost stalking this Nature's bounty. Taking pictures at various times and at various stages of the rich crop of mangoes, I sent them across to friends to share in this delight vicariously. To add the sound effects to this visual scene appeared the Koels indulging in a musical *jugalbandi* hiding in the green foliage of the tree with its resplendent crop. Begum Akhtar's raspishly sensuous voice in a plaintive lilting tune played in my mind: "*Koeliya Mat Kar Pukar…*". The tree weathered the early monsoon fury and the mangoes swung tenaciously from side to side like experienced trapeze artists. On sunny days the faintly yellow mangoes shone through the branches as if signalling to us humans to take the rough and the smooth with equal ease. Most of the mangoes have been harvested, and the cycle will play out every year only if we desist from destroying the fragile ecological balance on planet Earth.

Memory is not bound by a chronological timeline. It rewinds and fast forwards in a constant motion. With the enforced isolation amidst the quarantine time and space have stood still. A wrist watch, I realised, is merely a futile handcuff on time!

***

Ba-Ba Black Sheep!

Bad Boy Billionaires

An iteration of two simple syllables: 'Baba'. The familiar word has layers of meaning braided into our minds. It can range from the image of a Sufi mystic like Baba Bulleh Shah preaching love and brotherhood, the thought of a revered father addressed affectionately, the image of a lean mendicant Sadhu or just the sound of a child's prattle spouting the word with joy. And suddenly looms on the scene the much-in-the-news Yoga Guru turned business magnate Baba Ramdev! And the word Baba acquires fifty shades of grey.

Lovers of Asterix comics will see a similarity in this dhoti-clad Baba with the famous Druid, Getafix of Gaul. He with his flying cape and hair and the secret magic potion that gave the Gaulish warriors superhuman strength to beat back the Romans. Our very own Baba with his flying hair and dhoti has a magic potion too, Coronil, to battle the Corona virus. The secret ingredients of the magic potion made from the herbs around the village were only known to Getafix. Baba R too is the only one privy to the making of the Ayurvedic Coronil kit.

So far so good, but he excoriated the medical fraternity by 'rubbishing' allopathy as '*tamasha*' and calling the vaccine ineffective. This got the Good Doctors into a temper against these remarks that reveal his unscientific temper. The powers that be had to rap the gadfly Baba on the knuckles to take back his remarks. On the one hand the frontline warriors were being showered with petals for their dedication after the first lockdown, and now suddenly pelted with abuses. Baba Ramdev got his dhoti/ knickers into a knot there.

He was forced into tendering an apology and recanting the claim of the drug being an antidote to Covid. Ironically enough the honourable Judges from the Delhi High Court chastised the medical fraternity for paying attention to his remarks instead of finding a cure for Covid but stoutly defended Baba Ramdev's right to free speech. He smartly repurposed the kit as an immunity booster and got away with his tongue lashing of our good Docs.

Somehow the Yoga Guru has a record of being in sticky situations. In 2012, he got on the Anna Hazare bandwagon by joining the protests at Ramlila Grounds against corruption and for strengthening of the Lokpal Bill. He did a Houdini act of evading the cops by wearing drag. But to his great discomfiture the Delhi police was able to 'drag' him out of a cluster of salwar kameez clad women and lodge him in the clink. And all this on camera.

Unfazed he carries on as a self-anointed globe trotting Yoga Guru, with a massive Patanjali empire of consumer goods co-founded with Acharya Balkrishna. Media savvy Baba Ramdev uses social media to the hilt. A Grandmaster in brand building he has his own TV channels to spread the word. Lest you thought him to be our *Nukkad* Baba, Patanjali has even an ashram on a donated island in

Scotland. Any casting company looking for an update of the Netflix series, 'Bad Boy Billionaires'?

Curiously enough, he is eager to have the Patanjali products branded as scientific while heaping abuses on the practitioners of evidence based science and their products. Our traditional knowledge of Ayurveda is held in high esteem and there is no need to denigrate a parallel system of medicine to gain brownie points.

Babas, Gurus, Swamis and Acharyas have always dotted the mindscape of Indians. With myriad gods and goddesses, each with an individual portfolio, perhaps we need these intermediaries as navigators. But to tell the real from the fake will test our G.Q (gullibility quotient). Or else, there'll be plenty of Ba-Ba's to pull the wool over our eyes!

***

New Shoes: Old Memories

The Devil Wears Prada

I belong to yesteryears— only chronologically, I'd like to believe. The upside about being long in the tooth is to possess a rich bank of memories. Dementia permitting, one can dip into it at will. H.G. Wells wrote a novella, 'The Time Machine', about time travel in a device. But old age gives us an inbuilt time machine with a rewind and fast forward button.

Having ordered a pair of sports shoes online, the parcel arrived at the door in a day. It was certainly convenient and fuss free. But my mind took an Olympic leap to school days when shoe buying was a chaperoned event. Bata, the storied Czech company, was the leading brand in footwear, both leather and canvas. An Indian company Carona was a competitor in canvas shoes and carried on a 'product war' like the Coke and Pepsi 'ad -war' in recent times with Bata. Carona folded up due to family feuds but Bata forges ahead well-shod and 'fleet footed' even now giving 'Happy Feet' to millions around the globe. In the sixties one of their ads said it all about their being *numero uno*: 'First Bata, then School'!

Visiting the downtown Bata shop in Srinagar to buy the standard round-toed buckled flats one felt a palpable excitement. Being fussed over by the salesperson for correct foot measurements and prodded by the parent to buy a size larger in the interest of parsimony, there was drama in getting shod! Arriving at a modus vivendi one would go home triumphantly with the trophy.

I remember keeping even the cardboard shoe-box, almost like an installation, to keep the new shoes neat till they got nicked and the love affair lost its edge. But the luxury in snowed-out winter was the beautiful soft leather shoes one wore at home, fur-lined and embellished with exquisite crewel embroidery by the Kashmiri artisans. A warm memory for those who could afford. One also saw the sturdy mountainous Kashmiri labourer wearing dried reed grass sandals called 'pulhor' and carrying heavy loads in winter without a murmur. Apart from these and the 'fleet shoes' one remembers the ugly black gum boots one wore in the snow. It was great to have the knee-height protection from melting snow when the world was 'puddle -wonderful' and 'mud-luscious' as the poet E.E. Cummings wrote.

Evolving from quadrupeds, with natural padding, to bipeds human beings have over millennia covered their feet in variants of shoes as we know them now. Anthropologists have gauged from the shrinking toe bones in skeletal remains that humans started wearing shoes around 40,000 years ago. The Chinese women were subjected to the horrendous practice of foot binding at puberty for centuries to make the feet small, almost like a doll's feet. Three to four inches length was a mark of beauty but it sadly led to physical deformities. Fortunately this patriarchal practice of 'Lotus Shoes' was banned and the foot binding died out in early 20th century.

Shoes have very fancy avatars in this era of disposable incomes and brand consciousness. A Louis Vuitton, Gucci a Jimmy Choo or a Nike— one is spoilt for choice. A unisex covetousness for attractive shoes leading to shoe-fetishism is there for all to see. Imelda Marcos for one will be immortalised for her humongous shoe collection.

Lest we blame the shoes as greed enhancers, please remember that shoes have also been used from Biblical times as a protest tool. Many 'Shoe Gates' have been recorded but in recent memory the 'shoeing' by an Iraqi journalist at George W Bush is recall worthy. He threw both his shoes at the POTUS as his 'sole' weapon, who ducked them successfully! It is certainly a 'shoo-in' that footwear can not be ignored. Even the Devil wears Prada!

Recipe Please

Food Glorious Food

Purely conjecture, but probably when the Cavemen did a good barbecue after their hunt, the word went round echoing in the wilderness about the tastiest morsel and oral recipes were born.

'Recipe Please!'—is a plaintive cry heard across the culinary platforms on social media, in family groups, in dinner conversations and even at restaurants. Obliging Chefs tell you the ingredients and hopefully divulge the little tip that made the dish acquire the extra dash to be palate tickling.

Diane Kennedy, a 98 year old British food writer calls food— not just step by step recipes but socio- economic documents and records of ecological diversity. She thinks recipe writing is deeply undervalued as creative work. She has rightly put her money where her mouth is (or ours for that matter!) considering how food is so central to our existence. Not merely as plain sustenance to give us energy but the centrepiece of our gustatory satiation.

From royalty to the homespun *Dadi Ma ke Nuskhe* of the unsung housewives, recipe books are treasured. Salma Husain, a Persian scholar and food historian gave us a peek into the Royal Moghul *Degchis* by translating the original manuscript, *Nuskha-e-Shahjahani,* kept at the British Museum. The result was a delightful book called 'The Emperor's Table', delicacies for an emperor who was more of a gastronome than a warrior.

Recipe books remain the hot selling item in a publisher's stable despite the You Tube bonanza. An interesting nugget about the famous Agony Aunt of food-columns, Betty Crocker, is that she was a fictive character created by an American flour company as an advertising gimmick. Her viral popularity made her the second most popular woman to Eleanor Roosevelt. Such is the magnetic pull of food. Celebrity Chefs shine online and we even have robotic cooks producing a meal!

Food can be a political tool. A teaser for statistics -beasts to answer whether Kamala Harris's food video in Mindy Kaling's kitchen garnered her a sizeable chunk of women voters in her ascent to the VP's chair? And if Hillary Clinton's dissing comment in the nineties on stay-at-home Moms baking cookies dented her image by casting her as a latter day Lady Macbeth with naked ambition. Though our home-grown Bihari Nari, Rabri Devi, with her 'down-to-chulah' image and a delectable name to boot, rose to sit on the CM's chair with great ease.

The food scene has witnessed some fisticuffs over GI tags given to certain dishes owing to regional pride. Rosogolla led to 'mukkabaazi, between Orissa and Kolkata each claiming the provenance of the sweet. It didn't leave a sweet taste in the mouth. Finally both states have a GI tag for their variants to end the tug -of -war in a draw. No

Indian foodie will believe that the ever popular street snack Samosa has an Iranian origin, as Sambosa. No threat of nuking our Samosa however!

Only fine dining from powerful nations used to make the cut at the high table. It was unthinkable to have Nouvelle Cuisine rubbing shoulders with 'Panta Bhat', a rice gruel and a poor man's breakfast dish. Many variants of this soaked rice dish exist in India. Recently presented by a Bangla Deshi contestant in the Master Chef contest with panache as Smoked Rice, it is gaining a pedigreed status. Food snobbery lies in tatters. Panta Bhat is considered a Super food now, which it always was, because of its pro-biotic nature. The first woman Chef to get a Michelin star is a young Indian Chef in Bangkok. Garima Arora who serves simple Indian food run in an informal canteen style restaurant space called, Gaa. She has put Indian food on the global food-map along with a few innovative Chefs of Indian origin.

Food glorious food—for those with means is always on the front burner. Sadly, the spectre of malnutrition does keep hovering over the stoves of a sizeable global population though.

Now that is food for thought! Any recipes for a more egalitarian food scene?

***

Samavar: The Self Brewer

A Whiff of the Past

This brass 'Samavar' belonged to my mother's kitchen in Kashmir, as she bustled about making *kehwa* with its cardamom and cinnamonesque aroma wafting through the spout. 'Kehwa' is related to the Turkish word for coffee 'kahveh' which in turn might be derived from the Arabic word 'qahwa'.

This memory is braided with myriad vignettes of afternoon visits by aunts and cousins when kehwa was the chosen beverage. Conversations were light and colourful, like the wings of a butterfly, between each sip of the sweet brew. Giggles and full throated laughter ricocheted from the walls. Very often Sitara Aapa was also included in the light gossip through an open window overlooking the neighbour's wall. There were no walls and barriers to love's free flow. The old brass cups were ideal for keeping the green tea hot but one had to hold the cups with a small towel. And like 'chai-biskoot' one had *Kulcha*, or another bagel-like sesame round bread. With the storied breads of Kashmir we were spoilt for choice. The neighbourhood baker was always churning out mouth watering breads one could send for in a jiffy. All this was in the informal family room, next to the kitchen. It was basically a ladies *Kaffeeklatsch* to shed the monotony of the daily grind.

In our itinerant Air Force moves from place to place, my Samavar has been a treasured family heirloom. Around a century old by now, a little dented it still has a certain swag. The brass is a little tarnished with a patina on the lower fretted base. The lid of the charcoal funnel is missing yet it has a presence because of the memories associated with it.

Samavar has a certain uniqueness and yet a kinship with its kindred variations in various corners of the world. Samovar, a Russian word, it means a self brewer. It has found a niche in many parts of Eastern Europe, Persia, Turkey, Central and South Asia. But the credit for manufacturing beautifully crafted samovars in mid nineteenth century goes to two men known as the Lisitsyn brothers in the city of Tula in Russia. It is a city known for its metal workers and armaments From ornate to simple workaday samovars used in palaces, homes and, of course, in taverns with huge Samovars pouring out the tea with the hubbub of conversation around.

With the quickened pace of life, even the Samavar makers have bowed to modernity and convenience and made some electric Samovars like an electric kettle. Even in Kashmir it is the rural hinterland that sustains the old style Samavars with live coal in the central cavity with space around for water. With the Selfie seduction most people pose with the Samavar as a prop in Kashmir to flaunt the fact on social media that all boxes have been ticked. Mostly, it is bought as a souvenir to be displayed on a shelf.

But till my breath becomes air, this Samovar of mine will whisper many stories in my ears. Most of all it'll keep pouring memories of my mother and Kashmir into my mindscape— even though its days of making steaming kehwah are gone!

***

Global Issues: Hot Potatoes

AAP
© Shailendra '20

Modish Designs

Power Dressing on Political Ramps

Churchill's churlish comment calling Gandhi a 'half-naked fakir' remains distasteful to date. It is deliciously ironical that a dhoti-clad under-dressed leader made the over-clad mighty British Empire eat crow. Gandhi became a global icon, notwithstanding the proverb that 'clothes make the man'. His sartorial choice of dressing like a common man was a master-stroke in creating an instant connect with millions of Indians. That is what one could truly call power-dressing!

Indian leaders over the years have understood the power of the symbol. Nehru, a darling of the masses, despite his elite lineage shed his former grandiose western attire. He became a global desi with his *achkan* and *churidar* and the Gandhi cap. Nehru's *bandh -gala* jacket was a fashion statement globally. Mao joined the high table of political power dressing with his army-type Mao jacket —an early instance of Sino-Indian rivalry even in power-dressing. The Nehru jacket continues to make waves even now as the jacket with the mandarin collar— a happy resolution!

Modi set the ball rolling for the political ramp-show on his campaign trail in his immaculate half-sleeved kurtas further embellished by vibrantly coloured waistcoats. It was a political statement—no need to roll up the sleeves to get cracking. He was on his marks and ready to hit the ground running! More so, it became a trending fashion statement.

A sneak preview of Modi's sartorial skills was showcased at the BRIC summit. His dapper 'bandh-gala' suits with an 'open-throated' espousal of India's development put him robustly on a global stage. The U.S. trip burnished his image further with a Rock Star platform at the Madison Square Garden. By now the Force was with him. One could almost visualise the NRI's doing a *lungi* dance to the tune of *Chak de India* in Times Square!

No wonder at the famous breakfast meeting with Obama back home, clad in a monogrammed suit it was stylish swag with solid swagger. Offended by the Fendi-like price tag of the suit the Indian tongues clucked in disapproval. Though the auctioning of the suit for charity muted the negative buzz. And now the Modi shawl worn in Paris is going viral. Watch out Louis Vuitton, we are promoting 'Make in India'!

Arvind Kejriwal, the David of Delhi uses his trademark muffler and casual attire to be one with the *aam aadmi* and take on the Goliaths. The Muffler Man of AAP may not be modish but he certainly has a winning strategy in his dressing style in sync with the common man. Bonding with PLU's, (people like us) always creates a comfort zone. Aam aadmi too wants LLU's–leaders like us. Hence the perfect fit for Kejriwal.

Indian leaders have given us a gallery of attires with regional and ethnic touches. From the rustic to the exotic we have it all–from head-turning headgear in glorious colours and shapes to the simplicity of a dhoti kurta or the beauty of the handloom Sari. You could truly say—Fab India in more ways than one!

✷✷✷

Black Swan Syndrome

Game Changers: Trump, Brexit, Namo and Demo

Please note, it seems to be open season for global shock and awe! Britain severing its nuptial bond with EU sent more than ripples around the globe. Brexit was not the outcome expected by most—least of all by David Cameron. It was a black swan moment that turned out to be Cameron's swan song. Looks as if everyone read the tea-leaves wrong—despite the Brit love for *chai*!

Close on the heels of Brexit shock came the seismic American Presidential election results turning the U.S of A into the Divided States of America. Contrary to sure shot predictions, the voters pilloried Hillary instead of dumping Trump! This left a large swathe of Americans gobsmacked in utter disbelief. Political pundits and analysts had to eat humble pie after their oracle like divination about the end result in the race to the White House proved a dud.

Brexit referendum and the Yank election opera played out in full view of the public, rising to a crescendo over a period. Closer home in Hindustan we had a different script crafted in stealth and shrouded in total secrecy. The demon of demonetisation came as a bolt from the blue (or black, should I say?). It was an '*Aakashvani*' in more ways than one.

Namo thundered 'no-mo'! No more of black money that is. This sent the black sheep bleating in misery and scurrying for cover and the taxmen on a mission to uncover the hidden dirty money. There were certainly more than three bags full to mop up for the overworked bank officials. This 'surgical strike' (a phrase currently in fashion) on currency is supposed to suck out black money, put brakes on fake notes and cut asunder the terror-black money nexus. This is Modi's '*modis operandi*' (no misspelling there!) to take us a step closer towards Digital India and a cashless society. The rub in the ointment is that in this bloodbath the much touted *aam aadmi* has been rendered cashless. 'Note bandi' may be less painful than 'nas bandi' but you have to put your money where your mouth is. With the cash crunch that isn't easy.

But as they say in India – worry not, J-tech (jugaad technology for the uninitiated) operators have razor sharp minds and can work around any road bumps. Apart from *Kala Dhan* being made 'fair and lovely' through innovative bypasses there is already hoarding of moolah being done in the new high denomination notes. The middlemen from the parallel Dalal street seem to have a lot more street-cred than the regular guys. That is the way the cookie crumbles! Having smelt an opportunity to make a killing they must be singing the popular Bollywood song with gusto—*Aao saade naal tusi aish karoge, zindagi ke saar mazay cash karoge!*

***

International Yoga Day

You Are on the Mat!

Hold your breath and breathe out. With a global high-five, 21 June has been officially anointed as the International Yoga Day. Having somersaulted over the summer solstice (Times Square tribute to it notwithstanding), it has made a yogic leap over mundane and saccharine sweet days like the Mother's Day. It certainly has taken the sheen off the robust Father's Day because of the clashing date. The suffering gents, as usual, have been put on the mat!

With an imprimatur from the United Nations IYD has made a blockbuster debut around the world. Look at its sheer stretch— Mountain yoga on the icy heights of Siachin, yoga on water in holy Varanasi, boat yoga in Paris on the famed *bateau-mouche* and sea -yoga on the imposing *INS Virat*. The Air Force, of course, has been doing a kind of aerial yoga for years with its pilots doing loops, barrel rolls and spins in aerobatics with the concentration of a yogi. Picture post-card venues popped up from far and near on IYD— yoga under the iconic Eiffel Tower, yoga in the famous Angkor Vat temple, yoga by the Thames, yoga in Beijing and yoga in the Rann of Kutch. Even an impromptu Flash Mob yoga in malls gave it a hip touch.

With India as the lead choreographer, IYD has a brand new identity. From the low-key DIY (Do it yourself) practice to the razzmatazz of IYD, Yoga has muscled its way to the global marquee with no '*asanas*' barred. With a commemorative stamp and coins to boot IYD is trending hugely.

Always associated with the mystic East, it did create a buzz earlier too in the sixties with Beatles hotfooting to Rishikesh with Maharishi Mahesh Yogi of TM (transcendental meditation) fame. Feeling a little possessive about yoga with its provenance dating back to the pre-Vedic period and current glory, some want to claim a GI (Geographical Indication) copyright for it. Heady Champagne, Bordeaux and other IPR denizens would gladly raise a toast to the new entrant in their fold. Other wannabees of Indian soft power—like the Sari and suchlike, with their impeccable *desi* credentials would also be clamouring for international recognition of such magnitude. Shaina N.C. wake up and smell the roses or rather drape the Sari around the world!

What got the world really gobsmacked was the massive yoga demo at Rajpath. It was a grand spectacle where the customary 'gun-salute' was replaced with the 'sun-salute'. With a record-breaking mass of nearly 36,000 yoga practitioners on their individual mats and nationals from 197 countries, India made it to the Guinness World Records twice over. The choice of politicos to lead the yoga sessions at regional venues was a masterstroke. Well-versed in bending over backwards and capable of twists and turns in any situation, most '*asanas*' would be a cakewalk for them. As for the 'Surya-Namaskar', the worship of the rising 'sun' is a given in their repertoire of convoluted postures and posturing.

Despite warnings against the commodification (no pun intended!) of this knowledge system, one can see the glint in the eye of those who think this could be a marketing bonanza for yoga merchandise in India. Yoga mats, yoga Tee's and pants etc. have been money spinners in the U.S since decades. Cards with exhortations to do yoga can make the cash registers jingle even louder. With the pop T.V. Guru, Baba Ramdev as the brand ambassador for Yoga in India, we can all bend it like Baba. With the 'leg up' that it has got through the IYD endorsement, one can say that Yoga can look forward to '*acche din*' now!

***

The Writing On the Wall

The One That Was Never Built

Trump may or may not build that infamous wall but there is a tangible Wall of Anger rising all across the Home of the Brave and the Land of the Free. Alas! Now rechristened the Divided States of America. All right-thinking people are seething with a corrosive anger though the 'alt-right' Americans are hailing the Trump diktats. 'He Who Must Not Be Named' is throwing in more toxic stuff in the cauldron to roil the witches brew further! As the Witches in Macbeth intoned, 'Fair is Foul and Foul is Fair'. The writing on the wall is there for all to see but for the *Numero Uno!*

Building walls of the mind is far more dangerous than merely raising a brick and mortar wall. Mexicans have had a rich native Aztec cultural heritage. They have been reduced to a caricature as merely the Taco-Enchilada-Tortilla making culinary wizards. However, 'Tex-Mex' fusion cuisine tips the American hat to the Mexican sombrero. And can one ever have too much tequila?!Half a century ago the American Rock band Champs immortalized the Mexican national drink with the foot-tapping number 'Too Much Tequila'—a Grammy award winner. A musical salute again to the tiny neighbour. Now we have a big bully with a stick threatening the 'Bad Hombres' to stay away. Instead of making America Great, all the dissonance and disruptions are making America grate on one's nerves.

Politics has to rise above the art of the deal. Perhaps Trump needed to be an apprentice in a show on the art of diplomacy and governance. Braggadocio is not another word for competence! 'Realpolitik' and 'Real Estate' are different kettles of fish. Alienating the media is not what McLuhan would have approved of. How intelligent are you if you question your own Intelligence agencies!

Walls have been erected all over the globe. Some have led to violence over competing claims as in the the Wailing wall of Jerusalem. Trump's wall may well become the wailing wall with trade barriers imposed on goods. Goodbye guacamole!

Way back in 1963 John F. Kennedy famously said at the notorious Checkpoint Charlie on the Berlin Wall, *"ich bin ein Berliner"*. He was displaying a global statesmanship and metaphorically demolishing the wall much before it came to pass. Surely Trump is not envious of the Great Wall of China? As long as the Trump towers keep rising high in all parts of the globe things are hunky-dory. Walls of Babylon and the Ishtar Gate are wonders of architecture. Such a grandiose vision doesn't figure in Prez's scheme of things. Perhaps he should heed the ovoid wall-sitting character Humpty Dumpty in the nursery rhyme from Lewis Carroll's delightful book *Alice in Wonderland.* A fellow American, a pastoral poet from Amherst, wrote in a poem so presciently titled, 'Mending Wall':

Before I built a wall, I'd ask to know, What I was walling in or walling out,

And to whom I was like to give offence.

Something there is that doesn't love a wall.

But then, Robert Frost was not from Wall Street!

✸✸✸

Brexit Syndrome

A Messy Divorce

Brexit – a political hot potato—has a resounding global echo right now! Certainly a shocker for some and a triumph for others in England. As the irrepressible American wag Bill Maher put it, a Jane Austen fan no doubt, some voted with sense and sensibility and others with pride and prejudice. David Cameron, who put his head on the guillotine block, thanks to the referendum promise on the campaign trail, has a severed head now. Despite the pre-nuptials, this promises to be a messy divorce between England and E.U. Any possibility of kissing and making it up seems remote at the moment.

Closer home we've had the handsome (a mandatory prefix to his name) RBI Guv, Raghuram Rajan, wanting to leave for the groves of academe. But across the pond we have one gent in the guise of Bernie Sanders who, despite more than straws in the wind, is not an easy quitter. He wants to remain in the Potus race but will have to bow out in the end. He will use his trump card finally to support the lady.

The Exit syndrome has spread to other domains too. Is it a cascading psychological contagion? What does one say when the famed English football team falls by the wayside?

That too, to the first timers Iceland! As the T.V jingle goes, they can hum 'Ice Ice Baby' under their breath since they can't bend it like Beckham anymore. For the nonce, the Vikings are kings. Fortuitous that there was no 'barmy army' by way of native fans to create a fracas on the field for having lost to minnows! The coach, of course, is offering his head on a platter for this debacle. Another icon from the football field, Lionel Messi, the man with the golden boot, is in the exit mode. He wants to pay the penalty for not having cornered one for his side. He failed in giving the chill-pill to Chile, hence his tears for Argentina.

Brexit may have released a genie out of the bottle despite the referendum not being a fool-proof weather- vane to gauge which way the wind blows on a political issue. Some copycat reactions are already being bandied about. In the hurly-burly of life we tend to forget the final exit that we mortals have to face. We, of course, don't have the choice to remain —as leave we must variously. No referendum on that!

Please Note!

Digi-Money but Staple Sense

Give me a fistful of coins any day. Any shape, any metal will do. I would even gladly hark back to the old barter system. Or perhaps fast forward to the brave new world of 'smart money.' Anything is acceptable if one can avoid ferociously stapled bank notes. I can bet my bottom rupee (that is if I can prise it out of the stapled wad) that many of us are long suffering victims of this trauma.

Bank tellers hand you wads of pre-counted notes in various denominations with a great flourish. But it is only when you try separating a few notes from the bundle that you realise what you are up against. The other day I tried pulling apart the notes with all the strength that I could muster. An attempt at twisting the bundle clockwise and anti-clockwise, as I had seen some shop assistants do with nonchalance, ended in dismal failure. I pitted my entire body weight against the unyielding bundle to wrench it open till I was blue in the face. But the sheaf of notes was Tantalus incarnate.

Taking a deep breath I reassessed the situation. It struck me that one needed a minor tool-kit to open the dashed thing. A screw-driver, a brass paper knife and a sturdy pair of scissors were my weapons of assault. It almost made me feel as if I was breaking into a bank vault. Zillion metal clips pierced the notes from both ends. With my 'screw driver' technology I was soon able to push up the staples from the innards of the bundle. Very soon I had erected a bizarre metal architecture on top of the wad of notes. Arches and thin columns of staple wire protruded in twisted shapes as if paying obeisance to this temple of money!

In the onslaught on this filthy lucre, I ended up with broken nails, bruised fingers and what is worse—a bruised spirit. The notes, not in mint condition to begin with, looked tattered and mutilated.

I should look at the brighter side of the situation, I told myself. Perhaps there was method in this madness. Was this a subtle way of curbing the money supply to put the brakes on inflation? Or perhaps it was an indirect way of reinforcing the saying that the fool and his money are soon parted.

Whatever may be the hidden benefits of this practice of turning a wad of notes into a veritable Fort Knox. I would still make a humble request to the powers that be. Please issue a notice to the bank personnel, with a *Nota Bene* (N.B), to follow a simpler S.O.P. No not a standard operating procedure but a less ruthless 'staple operating procedure'. That would be a 'noteworthy' development indeed.

A Prayer for the Valley

Kashmiriyat in the Land of Rishis&Pirs

Zabarwan—the word has a masculine ring to it. The purple-green shadows and the dappled sunlight on these mountains press the rewind button on my memory spool, as I step on the soil of Kashmir. A subliminal cascade of images and emotions flashes incessantly on my mental screen, like a film projector gone berserk. The familiar cadence of the Kashmiri language being spoken all around adds a healing touch. The bluest of skies with powder puff clouds dotting its azure expanse forms a benign canopy. The air has a crackling freshness one wishes one could bottle as a keepsake.

I instantly feel the bond with the land of my birth and upbringing. We collect our baggage from the carousel and get into our vehicle driven by the ever smiling Shaukat. We head straight towards Tula Mula village driving past verdant fields and pastoral hamlets. Small contingents of boys and girls walking to school with a resolute tread pass us by. We are on our way to visit the revered shrine of Kheer-Bhavani, a must visit each time we come to the valley. At the entrance one can see the tall Chinars towering around the temple with their jade green benediction. An array of clay-diyas, candy pillars, offering of flowers and leaves with a jug of milky water is kept ready in a '*thali*' for the devotees. We buy our stuff from lovely Razia. The moment one speaks to her in Kashmiri, her eyes light up. She showers blessings on us and asks us to forget the turmoil of the past two decades and return to the valley to make the ethos of Kashmiriyat whole again. Evidently, she is not merely a saleswoman but a philosopher to boot!

We endorse her viewpoint by clanging the brass tongue of the suspended bell at the entrance to the temple. One can see the Sufi tradition of universal love and brotherhood in this land of Rishis and Pirs is still alive. Despite the hiccups now and then, a little finesse is needed not to tar every one with the same brush.

In a cottage at the foothills of the Shankaracharya temple we wake up to the muezzin's call to prayer. The hum of chanting in praise of Allah in the mosques in Kashmir is so reminiscent of the Hindu and Buddhist style of chanting mantras. It is this syncretic Islam that imparts such a unique colouration to the valley culture. On a day trip to Pahalgam we visit the ancient Mammaleshwar stone temple. A Kashmiri pujari assists us in pouring water over the 'lingam'. When I ask him his name, it is heart- warming to know that he is Ghulam Mohammad, a local resident! This is what makes Lal Ded, the mystic poet, call her Lalleshwari or Lalla Arifa, a common heritage of Kashmiris.

Jhelum, almost an Eliotesque sullen brown River God, seems to have a furrowed brow at the anger and the angst scarring the peace and harmony in the valley. On the placid surface of the Dal Lake the gliding shikaras move to the rhythmic plop-plop of the oars amid the swoosh of water.

A young boy plucks a lotus flower and offers it to us. His name is Irfaan and he hopes to match the cricketing skills of his namesake.

During the last three days of our stay in Srinagar, we pay our homage, as always, at Hazrat Bal, Chatti Padshahi Gurudwara and the rock temple at Hari Parvat. We even chance upon a beautiful church in Raj Bagh and go in for a quiet look. The earnest prayer on our lips at each of these places is that the turbulence, that crops up from time to time, should end and Kashmiriyat fully restored again. Are the Gods listening?

***

Jailhouse Rock

Living it up Tihar-Style

Think prison! Sure enough, the synapses generate a Pavlovian association of taint, crime and punishment with the word. Not following the Biblical edict of an eye for an eye and tooth for a tooth in this day and age, prison management is big-time into R&R — I am afraid not rest and relaxation from the prison-grind — but reform and rehabilitation of the inmates. A little opprobrium with the word 'inmates' there, as prisoners however high-profile, are not called residents as yet! Sweeping changes in these times of make-overs have given a new avatar to the prisons. They are no longer the dreaded abodes of yore spilling with gore.

As jails go, T.J (stands for Tihar Jail, for those not into nifty abbreviations) is a hip and happening place. News about T.J activities is splashed all over the national dailies. Handicrafts made by the prisoners are advertised in a catchy radio-jingle extolling the wide range of stuff. You can have your pick from biscuits, clothes, bags to furniture. The non-boutique price tags are a great draw. T.J has brand value now. From 'chic'anery to prison- chic — an amazing example of transformative handling of people of all shades. (No pun intended there!) The latest buzz is that the food court at Tihar is getting a make-over to become a trendy place for a convivial luncheon date!

The activities calendar at Tihar could be the envy of Page 3 glitterati. There is yoga for fitness and healing, painting and music for therapeutic self-expression, vocational training and motivational lectures to bring about a change of heart in those who have erred. To lend gravitas and legitimacy to the efforts of those in prison, exhibitions are held and inaugurated by celeb dignitaries. 'On-campus' recruitment for jobs by corporates with a social conscience, is the current buzz-word in Tihar. And there are enough skilled people inside being snapped up for appointments in a wide swathe— from tourism and computers to finance and business development. A door might have clanged shut on their freedom but a window has opened to give them a second chance. Though there always is a Jekyll and Hyde aspect of the prison yet it seems so well-run and positive that at times the world outside appears beset by murder and mayhem.

Those long in the tooth will conjure up images of martyrs and heroes, who added lustre to the prison by just being confined there. Yerwada Central Jail and Naini Jail fit the bill. Images of national icons and freedom-fighters like Gandhi, Nehru and many more, who made prison going a noble act, flash upon our mind. What is more, 'prison-lit' like 'chic-lit' is a sizeable body of writings. Apart from diaries and other literary outpourings of incarcerated people, Nehru's brilliant and sensitive portrayal of Indian history in *The Discovery of India* is a literary gem penned in Ahmednagar Jail. Gen-X recently savoured the fervour of jail-going through Anna Hazare's brief stint at Tihar in the crusade against corruption. With viral networking in this digital age, one saw civil-society morphing from "chatterati" to "causerati" with abundant '*Kolaveri Di*' (killer rage) against graft.

Elvis Presley, the King of Rock and Roll, in his inimitable voice made the song "Jailhouse Rock" a huge hit worthy of inclusion in the Rock and Roll Hall of Fame. It was his take on prison-life. Apparently the musically inclined denizens from the motley crowd at T.J had formed a Rock-Band called "The Flying Souls". A clear signal that though physically fettered, the souls could yet take wing on musical notes. Not just dulcet voices from prison, there happen to be nimble-footed dancing inmates in Cebu Prison in distant Philippines. They have made a viral video called "Thriller". So folks it is show time in the clink in more ways than one. Elvis the Pelvis would certainly approve!

IPL vs BPL

Hardly Cricket!

For a nation that eats cricket, sleeps cricket and dreams cricket, this 'match-fixing' between an IPL team and a BPL team is bound to raise not just eyebrows but howls of protest. Being such a high-voltage sports spectacle with 'high-vaultage' monetary returns, IPL doesn't need an introduction. In fact, now everyone wants a piece of the IPL cake by replicating it in their countries. But BPL is a grossly ignored, almost invisible, league. The abbreviation BPL stands for the Beleaguered People's League.

Though IPL T20 is a new kid on the block, we all know with our 20/20 hindsight that BPL has been a shadow companion for long. Before the legions of cricket junkies start baying for my blood to have the temerity to denigrate the great game by pitting Gulliver against a mere Lilliput, let me put in a disclaimer here to assuage their wrath. This is a fictive scenario of a match between IPL and BPL. Any resemblance to persons living or dead is purely coincidental.

(With due apologies to Salman Rushdie, the progenitor of magical realism and the darling of Lit-fests till recently).

The Mighty Daredevils and the Puny Baredevils are in the fray. The former team seems full of machismo; the latter looks lacklustre. The MD team members have the names of their sponsors emblazoned on their jerseys, bats, caps or whatever surface available. The 'body language' of the team is pure *'dabangg'*. On the contrary, in sync with their physique the Puny Baredevils are attired in an apology for a uniform. The PB faces wear a hollow look, as if to say, that the only fabric they have is the warp and weft of life—if that!

The skipper of the MD team comes on to the pitch dripping with self-assurance. The PB captain, as opposed to Captain Cool, gingerly steps on the field. The Mighty Daredevils captain wins the toss and decides to bat first. He struts past the PB captain and mutters something under his breath. Sledging is par for the course or the wicket one should say, except when you get on a sticky wicket using 'desi' cuss-words on aggro foreign players a la the turbanator Harbhajan Singh. That was a script tailor-made for a sports film — "Bhajji on the Field"—no sequel to the movie "Bhaji on the Beach" I am afraid. Though one must acknowledge that the feisty Zohra Sehgal, who acts in this movie, was capable of scoring a century on the field and off it. She nearly did!

Team MD has attractive cheerleaders rooting for their star-studded team, going into an acrobatic routine whenever the ball goes careening across the boundary. Team PB has only Cheer-less leaders and a gaggle of unkempt supporters clanging their empty tin cans. No wonder the question uppermost in everyone's mind is, 'What is a BPL team doing in a 'feel good' show like IPL'?BPL is a tear-jerker. It shows you the visage of deprivation. Who wants to hobnob with losers? IPL is an adrenaline pumping station with all its attendant hoopla whereas BPL reminds you of the dregs of life. In this age of 'laughathons' and similar fare, no one has the stomach for sob stories any more

The pitting of these two teams, the brainchild of the Department of Social Justice, is to bring a burning issue to the front burner. Though the Mighty Daredevils trounce the Puny Baredevils, the underdogs do deserve support and a leg-up not a leg before wicket. Perhaps the distress of the BPL team and the alacrity of the umpire to raise the finger on the players will rouse the slumbering goodness in people for a fairer set of rules. The Mighty Daredevils, as expected, amass a massive score and outclass the Puny Baredevils in all departments of the game. The PB's despite taking the bouncers on the chin are able to muster up a total of only 32 runs.

Sorry folks, no 'Lagaan' like twist in this tale. The underdogs need to be 'beefed up' to fight another day!

***

Kim and the Donald at the Global Table

Tweedledum and Tweedledee

What a jaw-dropping vaudeville performance on the global stage it was in the Trump vs Kim face-off! It was open season for dire threats (thankfully empty) and colourful taunts. Both remained undaunted by the verbal salvos fired at each other and an on-going war of words continued apace. We had a high TRP political Reality Show bordering on surreality. Was this a *trompe l'oeil* (Trump l'oeil-trick of the eye!) or for real?

To the utter delight of the Twitterati and other social media, a whole manufacturing industry of jibes and jokes was flourishing online as a result of this standoff. Mirror images of each other being full of swagger and endless braggadocio could earn this strutting duo brownie points from Don Quixote himself. Their inflated egos hovered over the world like an ominous mushroom cloud.

Trump and Kim seem to be *dramatis personae* in a Lewis Carrol tableau. They have shades of Tweedledum (Tweeter-dumb perhaps!) and Tweedledee in their clownish acts with a bit of Humpty-Dumpty thrown in for good measure, what with their fixation on walls. Trump by raising the

Mexican-wall spectre 'poll-vaulted' over the White-House walls and Kim the Korean was excoriating the Yanks counting on the Great wall of China.

In this evolving tango both had honed the fine art of heaping vituperations on each other. (to give plain abuses a semantic gravitas!) Trump, wagging his finger, called Kim the 'Little Rocket Man on a suicide mission'. Further embellishing the abuse, Kim was called a 'rogue and a gangster fond of playing with fire.' The riposte from Kim was equally toxic— 'I will surely and definitely tame the deranged US dotard with fire'. For a value-addition to this cuss-bank, the Korean foreign minister used a proverb to deflect the 'fast and furious' attack from Trump saying—'scaring us with the sound of a dog barking, that's really a dog dream.'

The Nuclear Club is certainly riled at the temerity of Kim Jong-un wanting to join this high-table. A bizarre scenario with sinister undertones unfolded in front of our unbelieving eyes. If Kim with his dangerous toys, in a mad act unleashes his cache of lethal biological weapons, the phrase 'a plague upon you' will not remain a mere curse!

Both Trump and Kim need to shed their schoolyard bully persona and not go ballistic in their language and missiles. A huge responsibility rides on their shoulders. This may smack of levity but perhaps Donald could use the googly of 'covfefe' (an incomplete tweet he used against the American press recently) on Kim the Dim to keep him guessing. Jong-un would certainly consider this a 'wrong-un'! Who knows his bafflement might defuse the grave crisis?

***

The Ministry of Utmost Cleanliness

With a Nod and a Wink to Arundhati Roy

My apologies to the fabled Arundhati Roy for purloining the arresting title of her recent book for a piffling piece like mine. But then I bank on the gravitas of the Hebrew proverb that places 'Cleanliness' next to 'Godliness' to give some heft to the subject. After a life time of dalliance with cleanliness and order, which went mostly unsung, I find myself unwittingly in sync with some trendy issues— national and global. So here I go with a nod and a wink to both Arundhati Roy and Marie Kondo.

Most of my young days on my train travels out of Delhi I was willy-nilly subjected to a ringside view of a row of anonymous derrieres near the railway tracks engaged in open defecation. Oblivious of the rattling trains and prying eyes this morning 'road-show' went on for decades. Cut to the present. With campaigns like "Nirmal India" and "Swacch Bharat" the dirty urban sprawl is changing ever so slowly but surely. Radio jingles and dedicated ad-spends on this issue are tackling the Beast of Filth with great vigour. Open defecation and toilets are no longer taboo subjects. In fact they are hot-button policy issues linked-in with women's empowerment.

What has taken this unmentionable subject to another level is Bollywood film directors stepping in to turn this into bankable movie material. Weaving in toilets as a love story, "Toilet—Ek Prem Katha" (2017), the most unlikely title for a Bollywood romance, starring Akshay Kumar was a box-office hit. Another movie, "Halkaa" (2018), has a boy in the slums of Delhi battling poverty and corruption to raise money to build a toilet for himself. Sensing the impact of movies with themes of this nature the latest entrant into this arena is a movie released in March 2019, "Mere Pyare Prime Minister". A touching plea by a young boy to the P. M. for toilets in Mumbai slums after his mother is raped in the fields while out for defecation at night.

Who would've thought that engagement with hygiene would bring international laurels to India. Guneet Monga, an Indian producer of a short documentary titled, "Period. End of a Sentence" brought home the Oscar in 2019. Highlighting the hush- hush subject of menstruation in rural India, the documentary shows how a simple act of setting up a vending machine for sanitary pads leads to gender eempowerment. Earlier in 2018, a mainstream bio-pic on the 'Padman', Arunachalam Muruganantham, had picked up the same subject with Akshay Kumar featuring again as a crusader for a woman's cause. It wouldn't be far-fetched to say that the Supreme Court verdict on the Sabarimala temple case allowing entry to women of all ages is the result of this discourse.

This new crusade for cleanliness, personal or general, will have a huge gender and social fall-out no doubt but it is manna to my soul for other reasons too. I suddenly find my self-esteem scaling new heights. Having been accused of Obsessive Compulsive Disorder Syndrome (OCDS) because of my fixation with cleanliness, I have the last laugh now.

My tenets of utmost cleanliness are government policy now. My obsession with order and decluttering has proved to be a money spinner for a Japanese housewife with similar fixations. Marie Kondo is a global Guru of Cleaniness and Declutter. She has shows streaming on Netflix and her books on the art of de-cluttering are on the best-seller lists. Though this does "Spark Joy" in me, I wish I had also learnt the art of parlaying my skills earlier!

Weighing in on Donald Trump

POTUS and the Hocus Pocus

This much is for sure that ignoring Donald Trump is a 'uuge' challenge! He certainly lends himself as a deliciously easy target to play darts on. Despite his lexical inadequacies, the colourful adjectives for his chosen adversaries ride the cyber waves creating great mirth. The all too familiar 'Crooked Hillary' during the Presidential campaign cost Hillary Clinton dear. His recent *'jugalbandi'* with Kim Jong-un yielded the nugget 'Little Rocket Man'. The latest addition is 'Sloppy Steve', reserved for his one-time BFF and strategist Steve Bannon. After eating out of Bannon's hands during the campaign Trump suddenly decided to put a 'ban- on' the old faithful. He decided to 'Alt- Right and Delete' him. All these catchy adjectives have an adolescent ring to them—but then nobody ever accused Donald Trump of being mature!

About time the POTUS "mulled" over (Robert Mueller, be warned!) the ongoing hocus-pocus about the Russian intervention in the recent presidential elections. Donald, as we know, loves to 'put – in' his foot in his mouth, so this trail might get hot (Watch out Putin!).

Melania is not a happy '*Dulhaniya*', what with Stormy Daniels brewing a storm with the leaked salacious gossip about Trump's peccadilloes. Not content with 'pussy-footing' (Oops! Not a kosher pun!) anymore, Melania made a solo appearance at the State of the Union address. Perhaps pondering over her own marital state of the union.

All the mud flung at the Donald makes him 'duck' with statements that are pure unadulterated braggadocio and bravado. Analyse this: 'I am a stable genius' as a riposte from Trump to the juicy allegations in Michael Wolff's hot selling book, 'Fire and Fury'. Sure he is a stable genius with such horse sense emanating from him. The only problem is to redefine both stability and genius. The Wanna Cry ransom ware that hit the computers recently was firewalled eventually, but what do you to a nation that chooses a Prez who makes them 'wanna cry'!

Trump seems to be caught in a time warp of the reality show, 'The Apprentice' that he anchored with great élan. 'You are fired', with the finger gun gesture after every episode, is still a favourite line in his White House avatar. Look at the stack of fallen angels. Quite a blood bath — from Generals, advisors to Press handlers amongst others. The capitalist author of 'The Art of the Deal' may have dealt out a pack of cards with too many jokers in it. Whatever happened to the trump card!

With Donald's unbridled Tweets on social media, the Twitterati doesn't know what hit them. Perhaps the time is right for compiling a book on the tweet- salvos fired by @ real Donald Trump at odd hours of the day or night. 'Thus

Spake Donald Trump' sounds like an enticing title. Once he gets his 'covfefe' right, perhaps the Americans can breathe easy!

✸✸✸

Egg On Your Face!

Diet Fads

Dietary diktats on what to eat or not to eat are thrown at us with every ping on our devices thanks to digital connectivity. One is bombarded with messages on health-foods, super-foods or else dished out veiled or overt warnings on toxic foods. Dietitians and nutritionists are the sought after celebs in this age of visual braggadocio on social media. No one wants to look less than perfect. Hence the obsession with fitness and food, apart from 'selfies'.

'Eat Right' is the new slogan. But the hapless consumer is faced with a barrage of diets. Hard pressed to take a pick from Low Carb or No Carb, Vegetarian Diet, Gluten Free Diet, Raw Food Diet, The Zone Diet, Mediterranean Diet plus many more leaves the baffled health- buff in a soup (if they are allowed to imbibe that!).

Yesterday's heroes strutting on the food table are today's villains hiding themselves under the table. Take the favourite on many a plate. Eggs were considered wholesome food for long. It seems, with ethics put on the back burner, the sugar lobby in the sixties paid scientists to declare eggs as a 'no-no'. The threat of high cholesterol led many an 'eggo-maniac' to avoid the 'ovoid' favourite. But new research, hopefully not sponsored by the poultry lobby, has changed the script again. The eggs have been given a good chit now. But like the 'Good Taliban' and the 'Bad Taliban', whites of eggs were kosher but the yolks were dangerous. Now there is a U-turn again and the yolks have been cleared of the yolk of villainy!

A host of other food products have been locked in combat for years. Take our daily beverage. Should it be 'Chai Pe Charcha' with its anti-oxidant benefits (political not counted!) or should we 'Come Alive with Nescafe' as the classic Indian ad prompted? You read the tea leaves and weigh your cup of tea or coffee and decide. Butter or margarine? These two were also adversaries in the nutrition world but finally the 'utterly-butterly' milk product has won the battle. Chocolate in its dark avatar has been declared as a remedy for cognitive decline in addition to enhancing longevity. Good enough reason for people to become chocoholics. Chocolates have not only been subjects of popular writing but some charming films too.

Even the cooking mediums have seen a see-saw. At the moment only the 'keen' mustard oil has mustered some muscle power against the much feted olive oil. It has finally offered an olive branch to it and both live in peace on the food platter. Fermented food is in but in our pursuit of Western haute cuisine we forget that our desi foods like idlis, dosas and other fermented stuff were always ahead of the curve born of native wisdom.

Way back in 2004, Gillian McKeith's television series on BBC, "You Are What You Eat" was hugely popular and was made into a film too. She stressed the importance of gut health. Closer home we have nutritionists like Rujuta

Diwekar who have a huge following through books, social media and lectures. Her star client is the Bollywood diva Karishma Kapoor envied for her size zero. She insists that there is no magic pill to get you into shape but an understanding of a balanced diet and your metabolism. Ishi Khosla, Shikha Sharma, Luke Coutinho and Ryan Fernando are also spreading the fitness mantra.

What to eat and keep fit is an obsession with the 'haves' but we must remember that there are still pockets in the world where people who lead hard-scrabble lives have worries on what to eat at all. The Global Hunger Index places India 103rd out of 119 qualifying countries. We are almost at the bottom of the heap. So eat right is alright but if we continue to do this navel gazing we will get egg on our faces by ignoring such a large chunk of hunger!

***

Corona

A Crown of Thorns

A nano-sized particle called Corona is on everyone's lips. Heaven forbid, not literally though! COVID-19 is a virus '*sans frontiers*' making a triumphal advance across the globe in 2020. No other word in recent memory has gone viral worldwide with such speed as this. Embellished with the adjective 'novel' as a prefix, Corona virus carries a spiky protein crown around its body, hence the royal tag. That crown of thorns is a thorn in our sides now. A puny pathogen, 100 million can sit on a pinhead, has the Homo Sapiens in its thrall. Having assumed a pandemic avatar, Corona virus, being a shape shifter, has made us press the panic button with full force now.

The novel Corona virus has an infamous lineage. SARS and MERS are its villainous siblings that also made a cross species jump. Corona was first identified as SARS-CoV and was reported in Asia in 2002 originating in bats. And now it has made a comeback as SARS-CoV-2 originating in a Wuhan wild life live market of bats, snakes and pangolins.

MERS-CoV spread its tentacles through infected dromedary camels to people in 2012. But 'mers-ifully' stayed confined to a limited area in Middle East.

Clairvoyants, psychics, film makers and writers have warned of a doomsday situation from time to time caused through an invasion by a gallery of rogue pathogens. With '2020' vision some people interpret the French physician and writer Nostradamus's cryptic quatrains in his book of prophecies pointing to this outbreak of the COVID-19 nearly five hundred years ago! Quite a bit of a stretch that. Sylvia Browne's book, 'End of Days' published in 2008 has certain lines that point to a pandemic similar to COVID-19. And Kim Kardashian sharing a page on Twitter from the book has certainly given it traction on social media right now. Bill Gates red flagged the possibility of a pandemic like this some years ago.

Movies like 'Contagion'(2011) showed a viral pandemic killing 26 million people globally. So did the movie 'The Andromeda Strain' (1971), based on Michael Crichton's book. Movies like these strike close to the bone in times like the current crisis.

Plagues, epidemics and pandemics are not new to mankind.

Cholera, Smallpox and Flu pandemics have wrought havoc on humans. HIV/AIDS is still riding rough shod over us. The infamous Great Plague of London in 1665 killed nearly a quarter of the Londoners.

Cynical memes giving side effects of social distancing imposed to arrest the spread of the Corona virus are clogging the cyber world in an unending loop. The internet is awash with Corona related humour. Forced to be in quarantine it seems the divorce rates in China have gone up. The upside, as some wag tweeted, is that Shakespeare wrote his play 'King Lear' during the plague. To which a pert reply in the comment thread says that Shakespeare had no Netflix to distract him.

The scientists around the globe are in a mad race to conquer this virus through a vaccine. Curiously enough the only conqueror of Corona virus so far has been Asterix in the storied comic book series. In the 'The Roman Chariot Race' published in 2017, Asterix and Obelix take on the masked Corona Virus and his faithful Bacillus in a chariot race across Italy set in 50 B.C and beat them. Rather uncanny that the current Covid -19 is so severe in Italy.

Some uplifting posts create a bond of global oneness in facing the corona challenge. The dolphins are back in Italy, though the Gondolas are missing. The skies are blue and the birds are chirping without the snarling machines in the air and on earth. Does this nudge us to wake up and and smell the coffee so that we can smell the Good Earth!

We have spent untold amounts of money to build arsenals and flex our muscles strutting on the global stage against enemy nations. Only if we had thought of taming our greed and living in a more sustainable fashion the planet Earth would remain habitable and safe. It is this hubris of human species to tame and conquer Nature and forget the interdependence of organisms that has muddied the waters.

In face of this viral challenge we need to unwind, introspect and rejig our lives. So no *'rona'* for Corona. Let me reach for a glass of Corona beer to unwind! The Mexican company is not changing its brand name despite the adverse association. Cheers to vanquishing the imposter Corona and live sustainably!

Lockdown Blues

New Commandments

SARS-CoV-2 strutting on the world stage, unseen yet deadly, puny yet puissant, fragile yet robust is planting its kiss of death all around the globe. The gloves are off on both sides—Microbes *vs* Humans— an old familiar story. A global race is on to decode this mutating microbe and find an antidote to knock it out of the ring. This deadly bout will be won too eventually but at great cost.

Yes there is an economic meltdown, a bloodbath in the share market, political churning, hunger and much more. The shock waves of being blindsided by this stealthy virus are ricocheting around the world. We certainly didn't have the 20/20 vision to see this 'bull in the China shop' approaching despite its cameo appearances in its two earlier avatars.

The fallout on mental health because of the fear psychosis of this invisible enemy has been serious. Social distancing and isolation required to keep the spiky spectre at bay has had its toll on individuals and relationships. The much maligned digital addiction has proved to be a saviour in this scenario of 'Home Alone'. Zoom parties are booming and internet memes on Corona are circulating in a ceaseless loop. Humour is an armour against fear. It is like whistling in the dark to garner 'pretend' courage.

My take on how to handle the 'con-jugal' co-existence after an online poll has made me formulate a few Covid-commandments, not carved in stone, to ride through this social distancing and prolonged proximity. Since in India we are even appeasing the planets on a national level, let us appease 'Mars' and 'Venus' before the marital relationship turns into a 'martial' combat. No gender bias, both parties have to resort to a *modus vivendi* to come out unscathed from this incarceration.

My commandments are based on my limited 'randomised control trial'. I tip my hat to the two Nobel Laureates, the lionised economist duo of Abhijit Banerji and Esther Duflo. They used this method for poverty alleviation solutions but mine was to find a way for conjugal conflict resolution. Certainly a 'Nobel' objective.

It struck me with force just now what a potent ambassador Amitabh Bachchan would make for a 'lockdown' motivational clip! With his famous line 'Lock Kiya Jaye' from KBC in his baritone voice, all Indians would swallow it hook line and sinker.

Since my opinion poll was confined to an urban middle class group of a certain age and generation, the solutions would not be totally applicable to the DIG yuppies. (Double income group young professional persons). So take your pick.

With the daily helpers also in lockdown the workload on the LOH (lady of the house) is huge. The biggest battlefield could be the kitchen. In the B.C. (Before Corona) period the man of the house avoided the kitchen as if the floor was laid with mines except for making an Olympic dash for a bottle of soda from the fridge. But in A.D (After Disease) 2020 he has perforce to help with the stack of dishes to remain a 'woke' male. A daily 'Soap Opera' plays out in most kitchens though. Katrina Kaif posted a short video clip on You Tube recently on how she is doing the dishes and sweeping the floor. So ladies send this KK tutorial to husbands who would gladly watch the clip along with watching the 'dishy' demonstrator rather than watching the dishrag 'Patni' in a dish-hevelled state. Pati, Patni aur Woh redux!

Some men believe they need a hazmat suit to protect them from the Kitchen Virus! And some demand a '*Tamga-e-Jurat*' for venturing into the new battlefield for 'mopping up' operations. A must follow commandment for LOH is no critiquing the man for wasting tap water, flaring gas while looking for a sauce pan.

I would advise men to follow Arvind Kejriwal in how to wield the broom to make a clean sweep. Tutorials anyone from Aam Aadmi party?

Please remember wives are not Alexa at your beck and call and also remember husbands cannot be a substitute for your maid though you may be 'made' for each other.

This may be apocryphal but a group called 'Anonymous Husbands in Lockdown' (They better remain anonymous!)

is conducting an online poll if the 'malady' is preferable to 'milady'. To be gender neutral there is also talk of a store recently opened where husbands are on sale! Long live co-existence!

Covidnama

A Tough Gauntlet

This is a chronicle of an imposter, a '*bahurupiya*' — a shape shifting ersatz emperor with a fake crown of spines that dissolve at the touch of soap! But the soap opera around the globe plays out with humans cowering in fear with face masks, gloves and sanitisers as shields against this invisible virus with a double-barrelled name: Sars-CoV2-19. We, the strutting humans, with an overweening belief in our invincibility over Nature didn't read the Wuhan tea leaves correctly. Our confidence lies in tatters by being felled by a tiny virus that continues its deadly march across the globe *sans* frontiers.

Three months of isolation by way of Lockdowns 1 to 3 has given us the options to be either contemplative monks or mental wrecks with the shock of isolation. It almost seems that God has assumed an Avatar as a Supreme Blacksmith and we are either in lockdown or unlock-down at His whimsy! Nature, unlike the humans, has been in full refulgence, and the animals on land and water have been moving about with an enviable insouciance! The melodious call of the Cuckoo and the twitter of birds outside is manna from heaven. Perhaps an indirect nudge to the 'Twitterati' on social platforms that trilling sounds are better than 'trolling' cacophony.

Now that we are in unlock -down mode, a backward glance at the last three months is an eye opener in many ways. Each one of us devised our survival kit to cope with social isolation.

Music, Netflix, Nature, Reading, Board games, Video games, Culinary adventures, Yoga — anything to get one's mind off this dragon! A global roundup of emotions experienced by humans during the Covid pandemic is difficult to capture. Hunger, deaths, job losses, the migrant marches of the 'Nowhere People' closer home, plus a total economic disruption all over the world have singed us to the core. Yet thoughts and lighter moments that kept one from succumbing to the anaconda like constriction of our lifestyle come to mind.

Our residential complex seemed like a ghost haunt. No one moving on the roads, no sound of children playing and being generally rambunctious, no mobikes revving down the road, no car engines thrumming to life every morning was quite eerie. I was happy even at the sound of the security guard pounding his stick on the road. The cars in the parking lot looked like multi-coloured metallic toys abandoned by bored humans. The bluest of blue skies, the greenest of green trees and a colour palette of coral red Gulmohar with the sunshine yellow Amaltas outside was enough to brighten any jaded spirit!

Food, always a mood enhancer, led to excessive gustatory yearnings in the lockdown resulting in embarrassing avoirdupois in many a folk. What remained slimmer than before were the newspapers that fell at the doorstep almost without a thud. Covid writing 'finis' to business as usual, led to virtual platforms zooming in with webinars, meetings, virtual parties etc. Students with their education interrupted had to switch to online classes. New abbreviations cropped up and WFH (work from home) is the new reality. Covid related glossaries are bandied about with ease because of the infodemic generated by the pandemic. Quarantine, Super Spreaders, Hazmat, Asymptomatic, Droplet transmission, PPE, N-95 (A mask that sounds like a highway!) roll off the tongue with ease.

On the home front the lockdown led to depleted or no domestic helpers. This led to many a non-chauvinist husband making their debut as dishwashers or helping in other chores around the house. Women with their habits of not wasting and re-purposing kitchen stuff can be confusing for any male, particularly those from the armed forces. My insistence on saving banana peels for whitening teeth, over-ripe papaya pulp for a facial mask left my better half flummoxed about what constituted legitimate kitchen waste!

This pandemic, a wannabe emperor of maladies, like many others in millennia before will be put in the Hall of Shame in history because of the havoc it wrought. Whereas the Mughal emperors Babar and Akbar earned a place in the Hall of Fame with *Babarnama* and *Akbarnama*: Alas! Covidnama can make no such claims.

The Generation Disconnect

Boomers vs Zoomers

Despite feel good clichés like 'Age is just a number' the world is fixated on youth. Everyone wants to drink the elixir of youth and be 'Forever 21' and look selfie-ready to flaunt on social media! The 'demographic dividend' (183 million people will be added to the working age group of 15-64 years between 2020-50) is a catchy alliterative phrase in the India story. This geo- economic wonder ingredient is considered critical in unfettering the India shining narrative. Millennials are certainly raring to go and take the country to another level aided hugely by technology.

How can we forget another strand in this narrative, the senior citizens, who are not so yesterday anymore?

The senescent are no longer willing to be mothballed till they meet their Maker, or count prayer beads to ensure that they get a berth inside the Pearly Gates. Nothing will deter their zest for life. Age is not a cage they say! Those pensioners who've lived a disciplined life are ready to shake a leg, however shaky it might be. Sixty is the new forty—according to the new non-ageist arithmetic of the movers and shakers. Gymming and fitness is the mantra, travelling in groups, learning new languages, picking up new hobbies and even dating anew is par for the course plus there are marriage websites that open up options of finding a partner. This has unleashed a clique of 'sunset industry' *wallas* who are laughing all the way to the bank.

The hip and happening youth may be all for 50 shades of grey with their adrenaline overload but the old and the grey are not lacklustre either. The youth resist the diktat of unquestioning respect for age, though India still retains vestiges of this point of view in pockets of its hinterland. To reduce the disconnect between the generations both sides have to take a step forward and not live in frozen silos of Boomers vs Zoomers. Just as ageism is to be avoided, demonising the young is unfair too.

YOLO (You Live Only Once) syndrome drives the young to keep looking for fresh pastures and yet they don't have to put their parents to pasture. This has generated a whole industry of old age homes, ordinary and luxe. The old people without means is another story all over the world. Left adrift living on charity or on help from Good Samaritans, bring to mind WB Yeats' vivid image expressing the helplessness and indignity of being old—

What shall I do with this absurdity...

Decrepit age that has been tied to me

As to a dog's tail?

But a few iconic golden agers take the sting out of being long in the tooth with their brimming energy. Since we live in an age of brand ambassadors, no one better than legendary Amitabh Bachchan who has the *chutzpah* to be a perfect fit to fill the slot. On the cusp of being an octogenarian, the sprightly star is still 'cool' with that unmistakable baritone voice. Rajnikanth, the Tamil Superstar, could give Amitabh a run for his money. To add more heft to the old brigade and dispel any gender bias, who can forget the uniquely charismatic and zestful Zohra Sehgal, who did not go 'gentle into that good night' till her last breath at a defiant 102!

A feisty tagline for the Old could be the in-your-face title of AB's film:

Buddha Hoga Tera Baap

✸✸✸

Covid Conundrum

Survival Strategies

A maelstrom of emotions has hit us hard since Corona upturned the world as we knew it. Churning up, fear, uncertainty, anguish, compassion, stoicism, despair see-sawing with hope, ennui and now a resigned acceptance of the 'new normal'— a phrase gone viral like Covid-19.

Grappling with this ghost in search of a host, there is a new global bond and resolve to take on this pandemic challenge. It is a survival tool for humans to always gather their inner resources to face any untoward calamity. Heartening to see that there is an upsurge the world over to find ways to vanquish this invisible adversary. A cure at all costs with scientists racing against time is what we await with bated breath but even professionals from other fields are thinking out of the box.

Amazing to read that a retired engineer of Fiat, undeterred at the age of 86, has devised a kettle -sized gadget that sends air currents in the room to dispel the droplets suspended in the air when people speak. Age no bar! There's no stopping the gent who calls his device, Bio-Stopper. Not a cure but a safety measure for sure.

Repurposing, another Covid buzz-word, of drugs is another imaginative way being used to save lives. With hand washing as the main weapon against Covid-19 (a name that curiously could pass muster as a strong password) who better than Lady Macbeth from the pages of the Bard to promote this act!

She washed her hands out of guilt, we've got to do it out of necessity. "All the perfumes of Arabia, will not sweeten this little hand", she lamented. All we need to destroy the spiky corona is a bit of soap and water.

Masks have been used in various climes for many purposes but now in Covid times the masks are a must in public. From basic home made ones to designer masks, the mask making is gaining momentum in innovative ways. Even our homespun *Gamcha* is being modelled as a mask by no less a person than our P.M. and many others in the hinterland. It seems the apparel makers are making a 'Trikeni'— bikini with a matching mask! With PPE's and face-visors human beings have started looking like astronauts. The makeup industry is clucking its tongue in dismay at this quarantine scenario but its lips are sealed in more ways than one. The mask covers half the face, so read my lips if you can. No need for lipstick

***

Harris'd by Kamala

Donald Finally Trumped

It is open season on politicians in the election safari in the land of the free and the home of the brave! A battle of the ballot between the Elephant and the Donkey. In the tug-of-war ranged against each other are Trump-Pence vs Biden-Kamala duo.

Donald Trump may call her 'phoney Kamala' with his penchant for coining spiteful phrases but Kamala Harris is going to get under his skin. She is the new lotus that'll grow un-besmirched in the 'swamp' that he tom-tommed to drain. Time to chant the 'Lotus Sutra' for his redemption from spreading lies. This lotus is of Indian origin but nurtured in the American soil.

So he'd better say 'Howdy Kamala' now and see the elephant in the room rather than the one on the Republican banner. And the writing on the wall that he never built. 'Sleepy Joe and 'Phoney Kamala' are just petulant additions to his ever-widening vituperative vocabulary. We could come up with some of our own catchy phrases like 'Tweeter Trump' with his 'covfefe' moments, or 'Hustler at the Hustings'. But Kamala, without mincing words, called him a predator and there is nothing phoney in that.

Make no mistake! It is 'Chitti Chitti Bang Bang' versus 'Chitty Chitty Bang Bang'. This 'Tam-Brahm' lass has the chops to bleed the Republican duo. She has the organic colour of 'Bleeding Madras', a fabric originating from erstwhile Chennai and quite popular in America. And with a dash of the Caribbean gene pool she is the woman of the moment for an America riven by colour and identity.

Franklin D. Roosevelt, a well-loved President, is remembered for his 'New Deal' which pulled America out of the Great Depression in the 1930's. Alas! Donald Trump has only a nostrum purportedly for making America great again. In truth all he wants to do is to extend the realm of his real estate holdings that are assuming 'surreal' proportions.

In a co-authored book called, 'The Art of the Deal' he reveals himself as a shrewd businessman turning everything into a transactional bargain. Donald Trump belongs to the Nursery Rhyme World of Old McDonald's Farm. He would shine in the company of kindred ducks each quacking louder than the other. And he, of course, would be the most strident of them all to add another point to his brag sheet.

With experienced and compassionate Biden by her side, the rules of good governance will be rewritten. Biden has been 'biding' his time. And he is the man of the moment to unite Americans. The voters need the 20/20 vision to know fake from real to seal their destiny one way or the other. Trump has created a 'trompe l'oel' to create an illusion of he being the Saviour to save America's Soul. The time has come, as the Walrus said, to endorse the Abe Lincoln statement that 'you can not fool all the people all the time'!

✱✱✱

Singhu is King

Dilli Dur Ast

An inconclusive marathon '*Kabaddi*' match between the farmers and the *Sarkar* is playing in full view of the Indian nation! And now it is the cynosure of global eyes too. With families of Punjabi farmers spread across the world, the moral support is brimming from California to Canada and from Manchester to Melbourne. The tiller's connection with the good earth can never be sundered.

The peaceful protests at the borders of our capital city refuse to be washed or wished away with water cannons. It will not be 'contained' with a blockade of 'containers'.

The Punjab farmers are out in full strength at the borders braving the winter chill at Singhu, Tikri and Chilla, and many more entry points to Delhi. So Haryana, Rajasthan and U.P. farmers along with some from Tamil Nadu are all standing united in their protest against the new farm laws. Maharashtra farmers have called for '*Chalo Dilli*'. Sleeping in their tractor trolleys or under the trucks or in mushroomed tents on the roads, the protestors are unfazed. They are the true salt of the earth. Sadly some have even died because of intense cold or accidents on the way, but all this is borne without any rancour. So intense is the empathy for the cause that a Sikh preacher from Karnal shot himself dead unable to bear the pain at Singhu. This is 'Udta Punjab', not of drugs and degradation, but an Udta Punjab flying high with solidarity and determination.

There is a unique flavour to the farmers' protest. A *'Desi Tadka'* all its own, that can never be replicated anywhere in the world. No rural-urban divide here. Sharing food without class consciousness and a steely resolve to carry on no matter what is overwhelming. Women and children have also threaded together a support system by pitching in to help whichever way they can. All this has earned them huge respect. Now even the non- tillers from diverse fields are joining the protests in open admiration. Poets, artists, national awardees in sports, actors and just common people are lending their support. The golden tenet of Sikhs to volunteer help, *kar seva,* is in full play. Volunteers run laundromats, clinics and foot and back massaging services for the old.

Even a 4-page bi-weekly newsletter in Gurmukhi/Hindi called '*Trolley Times*' and the constant sustenance of *langars* carries on with clock-work precision. Humanity at its best!

People-power pitted against State-power in our vibrant democracy needs a dialogue to be scripted anew. All that the farmer wants is a sympathetic ear to assuage his fears. Speak to him without condescension and he will understand.

It is the robust and hardworking Punjabi farmers who rid us of the image of India sustaining itself on ship-to-mouth wheat imported from America under PL-480 until the sixties. Being branded as *Khalistanis* at these protests is indeed an unkind cut. To add insult to injury, the social media trolls bemoan the fact that the farmers were served a pizza *langar* by some volunteers not in keeping with the farmer's image, whatever that means. Unbeknownst to these uninformed trolls, pizza, with a wheat base, originated in Naples, Italy as a quick food for the poor working class there.

The negotiations with the Centre in a logjam so far, we may just have a new referee to blow the whistle on this tied tug-of-war. The Supreme Court has stepped in to resolve this impasse by suggesting an experts' panel to examine the demands on both sides. The farmers are earthy, tough and call a spade a spade. So any obfuscation and a rigid stand will not work. Reaching out, will. Singh was always King but 'Singhu' is a close competitor now!

✷✷✷

Take the Exes. Com

Spouses on Offer

This quirky title is enough to make many eyebrows go up in dissing me for my 'espousal' of the 'spouse swap'. Breathe easy, my intentions are totally in sync with the dire need to reduce one's carbon footprint by recycling. So let's chant the mantra, ricocheting around the globe, of up cycling to save the planet in diverse ways.

Why not apply this concept to marriage?

I know the counter question hurled at me by stats -beasts would be that marriage is going out of fashion globally. The wedding vow of 'till death do us part' is so yesterday and 'they lived happily ever after' is a feel good phrase found in fairy tales. Single by choice is a growing demographic. Even in the Indian patriarchal society there are more single women than at any time in history According to Pew Research Centre,38% of American adults between the ages of 25 and 54 were not married and a similar trend was evident in a study of many other countries. Riding on this wave there is a popular website for merchandise called, 'Happily Unmarried' which aspires to be India's coolest company.

Millennials everywhere are upending the old concept of marriage. From live-in partners to no strings attached attachments— all is possible. The newest threat to matchmaking sites is the concept of 'sologamy' (self marriage). A few young girls in India have recently tied the knot to themselves. If that sounds unusual, a thirty eight year old Japanese guy married a fictional character, Hatsune Mika, a virtual idol. He calls himself 'fictosexual'.

But fear not, I am ideating for some canny yet empathetic entrepreneurs to set up a portal for ex-spouses on offer. It could be a brilliant niche for ending jaded relationships by shuffling the cards. Voila! You have a second innings. The site should have services open to all gender fluid combos without bias.

This is also a piece of received wisdom that married people live longer. Hence the abundance of matchmaking sites like Shaadi.com and others. One goes by the intriguing name 'Footloose No More', which sounds more like a veiled threat of incarceration!

Now one could persist in asking why would a divorced person plunge into another liaison? Once bitten twice shy doesn't apply here, particularly in the celeb world of stars and starry folks. Hollywood actress Zsa Zsa Gabor had nine husbands and the storied Liz Taylor was married eight times (twice to Richard Burton). These two could easily be the poster girls for this site and to bring gender parity one can include the Twitter musketeer, the much married Elon Musk! A handful of Bollywood stars like Kabir Bedi and Amir Khan have also tied the knot more than once. So all in all a site for offloading exes could be a winning idea.

P. S. This idea germinated in my mind after seeing an Instagram site that recycles pre-loved Saris. So why not market pre-loved spouses?!

***

A Survival Toolkit in C.E (Covid Era)

Find Your Ikigai

To quote Don Quixote, the famous Knight created by Cervantes, in support of sanity may seem quixotic but it really isn't:

"*Too much sanity may be madness, and the maddest of all, to see life as it is and not as it should be.*"

That seems comforting advice in Covid times. It is not easy to have a 'lightness of being' with told and untold stories of loss and sorrow swirling all around us. But excessive emphasis on 'Gravitas' is only going to plunge our feet deeper into the morass of anxiety and depression.

We should be buoyed by the heart-warming stories out there to cancel out the horror stories of greed and gouging even for life saving equipment. See life as it should be as the Knight says. A certain amount of 'levitas' as opposed to gravitas (pardon my irreverent coinage!) is a must too.

I am not aspiring to be a life coach, be assured. My survival kit for sanity has a set of fairly easy and effective tools. Top of the shack-tool is the simple act of a full throated laugh.

I feel guilty about my erstwhile disdainful sneer at the laughter clubs sprouting like mushrooms in every colony. What I thought was a motley collection of oldies guffawing without rhyme or reason is actually a social therapy session. Being older and wiser, I realise laughter clubs are no laughing matter! John Milton's lines from the poem, 'L'Allegro' come to mind.

'And Laughter holding both His sides'

Laughter being the best medicine is a proven fact. Even the laughter induced by the Tik Tok funny videos with canned laughter, Snapchat, WhatsApp jokes and the ceaseless loop of memes can increase our happiness quotient. When the world itself is considered a 'Divine *Leela*', a playful sport, taking ourselves too seriously seems laughable!

Tool number two in my coping kit is to keep alive the sense of wonder. A tough task this, but worth following. The child in you should always lurk at the back of your mind peeking out now and then. Don't get too browbeaten by admonitions to act your age. Be yourself and revel in the moment. 'Mindfulness' is a money spinning global movement nowadays. You have to watch a child at play and you get your free lesson. Perhaps an imaginative engagement with whatever one is doing is the way to go.

With Covid lockdowns the outside has stepped inside. WFH (work from home), On-line Education, On-line Shopping, OTT platforms, Live Streaming Music, Virtual Theatre and Museums, even Digital Travel, Spectator sports without spectators, unthinkable earlier, are all clamouring for digital space. A whole new vocabulary has come into being.

The world wide web is a great gift but don't succumb to social media as a finger-wagging Nag at less than perfect posts. The danger of us becoming digital Hobbits is real! With the all-pervasive AI, our natural intelligence is imperilled. App-iness may just turn us into Androids.

So, one has to keep one's mind ticking. Many options exist despite our being locked in. Connect with Nature—curtailed through a window-view though, Sudoku, cross-word puzzles, board games, reading, writing, singing, meditation, Netflix or whatever gets you energised. Adopt the amazing Japanese concept of *Ikigai* in your work ethic. It literally means your reason to be.

Perhaps I got the survival strategies order wrong. Most of all we must express gratitude for each moment and day that goes by. Hubris for being *homo sapiens* has to be shed to be part of the oneness of this fragile planet.

Cannibis Indica

Dum Maro Dum

Cannibis indica, the euphonious Latin name for Bhang (marijuana) is a pointer to its hoary history in India. It has been called the 'food of the Gods' from Vedic times and is braided into the lives of the people. Holi and Shivratri would be mirthless without bhang *pakoras* and *thandai*. Lord Shiva, was partial to bhang. It was not '*rang mein bhang*' for Shiva, but its flip side— *bhang mein rang*. So the breaking news that Thailand becomes the first Asian country to legalise Marijuana won't cause such a frisson on the banks of Ganges where the Chillums are still being puffed with pleasure since time immemorial.

Legend has it that Shiva slept under the Cannabis plant and on eating its leaves in the morning felt very energised. Another charming story narrates the tussle between *Asuras* and *Devas* for extracting the divine nectar for immortality. Shiva drank the poison *Halahala* that emerged after the churning of the seas. His throat turned blue and Shiva became *Neel Kanth* adding yet another name to his awesome collection of titles. Mahadev was a 'cool dude' way before Millennials appropriated the term. No 'Superman' can top this 'Super God' with a Third Eye. And one with a 'boho' appearance and the ability to roll a 'spliff'!

In Atharva Veda cannabis is listed as one of the five sacred plants on Earth along with Tulsi, Sandalwood, Jasmine and Neem. This 'happiness weed' spread far and wide. Nizari Isma'ili in 11th Century Persia smoked hashish while invading the Christians during the Crusades. They were called Hashishins from whence the word assassin. Sufis, African cults and the Jamaican Rastafari smoke cannabis as an article of faith to create a mystic vision.

Sixties were the golden era of Hippies, the counter -culturists who made it cool to smoke pot and delve into oriental mysticism. College dropouts made Haight-Ashbury, a San Francisco neighbourhood their Mecca for hanging out.

The first Woodstock Music and Art Festival held in August 1969 on the East Coast over four days, in a field owned by a local farmer, saw a gathering of half a million hippies. They listened to Joan Baez, Jimmy Hendrix, Janice Joplin and many other iconic singers in a haze of hashish. Our own Sitar maestro Ravi Shankar too mesmerised the listeners with his magical playing.

It was the British rock band 'The Beatles' in the sixties that attracted more proselytes to this 'non-trad' lifestyle. They visited Rishikesh in 1968 with an entourage of high profile friends that included the actress Mia Farrow. To practice transcendental meditation ™ under Maharishi Mahesh Yogi and soak in the peace was their express intent. George Harrison learnt to play rudimentary Sitar under Ravi Shankar for a while. Unfortunately, there was trouble in paradise because of allegations of inappropriate behaviour against the Maharishi. The Beatles left variously much earlier than three months decided upon. This phase was their most creative and the classic White Album carries eighteen of their compositions. This includes a number that openly castigated the Maharishi in a song titled 'Sexy Sadie' that tarnished his image as a global guru.

Bollywood also tuned into this 'happy' theme in the movie, "Hare Rama, Hare Krishna" made in 1971. Zeenat Aman gyrating to the tune of 'Dum Maro Dum' in a smoke filled pub still attracts Likes on social media. Globally there are moves to make Cannibis legal medically and also for recreation with some mandatory restraints. Hollywood celebs like Justin Bieber are endorsing the weed in business ventures with legit companies. Bieber is truly in a 'joint venture' with a company in California to market pre-rolled premium joints named after a song of his— 'Peaches'. Many others are endorsing the use of therapeutic cannabis.

May be our Sadhus with their dreadlocks and ash smeared bodies and chillums could make an exotic brand endorsing the weed with the name— you guessed it— 'Nirvana'! And the tagline *'dum maro dum'*.

***

The Fevicol Moment

Fixing a Fractured Globe

Not just our beloved Bharat but the whole globe is in need of glue! This would be the perfect moment for the reincarnation of the famous Gaul, Getafix, of Asterix comic series fame. If ever India and the world needed a 'Fevicol moment' to bind its fractures, it is here and now—to give the adhesive brand its due for some delightful ads that 'stick' to memory for their humour and insight into our unique culture.

A *padyatra* that aims to connect with the people at grassroots level, whatever the political aim, is certainly worth every step taken. Aam Aadmi is the *Vox Populi,* to give a grander name to the voice of the people. And that voice has to be heard directly and not filtered through an echo chamber.

Wanderlust piqued the minds of many an adventurer, explorer, merchant and pilgrim in times of yore from lands far and near. Some came on foot, some by sea. The mighty Himalayas were no barrier to legendary travellers who came on foot. Ptolemy, from Greece, was here in AD 130 and wrote a geography of ancient India.

Fa-Hien arrived on foot in AD 405 across the icy desert and rugged mountain passes. Being a Buddhist monk, he went to Lumbini and other places associated with Buddhism. He learnt Sanskrit and took Buddhist texts from India for translating, having spent twelve years in India. Hiuen -Tsang also a Buddhist monk, came in AD 630 and stayed on for 15 years, out of which he spent four years studying Sanskrit, logic and Buddhism at Nalanda for four years.

Al-beruni, a Persian scholar and a polymath, came to India in 1024 and hung on for six years. He is considered a pioneer in Indology, being the first Muslim scholar to study India.

Marco Polo, the Merchant of Venice, was in India from 1292 to 1294. As a child he had been fed travel stories by his explorer father. He marched on the Silk Road for four years before reaching China and incredibly enough traipsing over the world for 24 years with his father and uncle.

It was his travel accounts of China and Asia that inspired others to follow in his footsteps. Coleridge's dramatic poem 'Kubla Khan' is inspired from Marco Polo's narrative on the grand palace of Kublai Khan of Zhengdou. It begins with the lines:

'In Xanadu did Kubla Khan, a stately pleasure dome decree—'

Ibn Batuta, came to Hindustan from Morocco in 1333 during the reign of Tughlak and stayed on for nine years. A Portuguese voyager, Barbosa, arrived in India in AD 1500 and spent 16 years, mostly in Kerala.

Then there were English and French travellers who came during the Mughal period and wrote accounts of social structure, customs and also about the flourishing trading ports at Surat, Broach, Cambay etc.

And the word spread of the storied wealth of India — its gems and diamonds, gold and silver, the spices and its art and culture. The vivid travel accounts of Oriental wealth propelled some countries into getting a foothold first and then becoming conquerors to plunder the wealth that dazzled their eyes. A perfect Arab and the camel story. And the rest is history!

With instant connectivity now, the mystique about other lands has diminished a great deal. From the North Pole to the South Pole the world is polarised in more ways than one. Wherever one looks one sees religious chasms, political fissures, wealth inequalities, racial discrimination, yawning gender gap and warring nations over territory displaying a brutal streak that is toxic and regressive. Let us be cohesive if not adhesive!

Let us travel in the way the mystic Sufi poet, Rumi said:

"And you? When will you begin that long journey into yourself"?

Bharat Jodo Yatra is in a continuum of earlier journeys undertaken in our country inwards or outwards.

***

Sheroes:
Woman Power

No Pot, No Knot

Toilet Ek Prem Katha

Women's empowerment is the buzz-word in contemporary gender discourse. Feminists of all shades talk of gender bias stridently in international forums. But far away from the glitz and glitterati, it is the women in a tiny district town near Bhopal who have given 'sisterhood' a new meaning by throwing the gauntlet to the male of the species. Young women refuse to tie the knot with someone who believes that the call of nature has to be answered in the lap of nature. 'No Pot, No Knot' is their resolute cry. It may seem a peculiar matrimonial requirement but awesome in its impact. Happily enough a *sarkari* scheme is giving some heft to this attempt at building '*nari shakti*'. The local administration has decided to conduct mass-marriages, called '*Mantri-Kanya- Daan*', only for grooms who can give pictorial evidence of being in possession of a proper toilet at home. The 'bottom' line is that these simple women are finally able to kick the male butt in the right direction — that of the toilet!

Glorious tales of royal '*Swayamvaras*' from our epics are etched on our minds. Lord Rama's prowess in being the only suitor who could lift Shiva's bow won him the hand of Sita. Arjuna had a more complicated condition to fulfill to marry Draupadi. He had to hit a moving fish-eye with a bow and arrow taking aim at its reflection in water. What these ordinary women in our rural hinterland are asking of the suitors is easy as pie compared to their royal sisters in days of yore.

An off the cuff remark made by a Union Minister recently that India has more temples than toilets created a brouhaha. He was accused of denigrating our spiritual heritage by equating temples with mundane toilets. But he was spot on in highlighting the dire need for more toilets by creating the '*Nirmal Bharat*' campaign to rid India of its image of a land of alfresco ablutions. A Bollywood diva, Vidya Balan, as the charming Sanitation Ambassador for the project has been helping in erasing this 'dirty picture' through a charming ad.

Sulabh International, an NGO, renowned globally for its *Sulabh Shauchalaya* and other transformative social projects is walking the talk to spread this awareness. To add a piquant touch, Sulabh set up an international museum of toilets at Palam in Delhi which houses a collection of toilet seats from different eras. Interestingly enough the museum has the replica of a throne- like toilet seat used by King Louis the XIV. He apparently held court unabashedly while sitting on the toilet.

One of the key reasons for girl students to not attend school or drop out is the lack of toilet facilities for them. In schools covered by the Right to Education Act less than 50 per cent have proper functioning toilets for the girl students. We need to realise that a simple measure like providing a toilet will eventually lead to more female literacy. It will create a generation of young women who are not merely abstract statistics in the oft-touted 'demographic dividend' of India. They will learn good sanitary practices thus ensuring a less disease prone life and in the process make a stellar contribution towards building a clean and healthy India.

Our dear old Bapu, the Father of the nation, insisted on the importance of clean toilets and cleaned them himself. We need to take a leaf out of Gandhi's book and endorse the fact that clean sanitary practices have a slew of dividends. Men may have finally met their 'Waterloo', thanks to our rural sorority in insisting on the need for toilets at home. The macho males have to admit that they have to mind their 'P's if not their 'Q's to woo the lady.

***

Divas All

No Glass Ceiling for These Feisty Ladies

The first woman prime minister of Britain, went gently into that final good night. Known as the Iron Lady in her heyday, she disproved through personal example the citing of the 'glass-ceiling' as the usual suspect in blocking a woman's ascent to the topmost echelons. True as it may be to some extent, there is a large and feisty gallery of women who have shattered the glass ceiling into shards and are shining worldwide in diverse fields.

Sheryl Sandberg, the chief operating officer of Facebook has created a buzz in feminist and other circles with her book, "Lean-in: Woman, Work, and the Will to Lead". Her book is the new feminist manifesto in the hugely networked digital age we live in. She believes that a woman needs to have a new mental template instead of pouring herself into a preset mould. As Gloria Steinem said, "I have yet to hear a man ask for advice on how to combine marriage and a career". The double X chromosomes create an impressive combo of intellectual and emotional IQ that can give a woman a definite winning streak on a level playing field.

Politics is one domain which has a rich harvest of outstanding women. Some of whom get a leg up because of dynastic connections but many make it to the top because of their grit and ability. Many political divas all over the globe and closer home have operated with weapons-grade sharpness. Maggie Thatcher could be a virago to forge ahead on her chosen path. Golda Meir of Israel was called the 'only man' in the Cabinet. (A rather left-handed compliment that!) Srimavo Bandaranaike with her homely appearance could manage an island nation with deftness. Benazir Bhutto with her oratorical skills and aplomb could hold a fractious nation together. Corazon Akino won the hearts and minds of the people of Philippines with her sincerity and passion. Eva Peron of Argentina shone like a star. And who can forget the steel magnolia from Burma, Aung Saan Suu Kyi, who chose her country over her personal life?

Angela Merkel of Germany occupied centre-stage in the E.U. configuration. No one but no one can beat the British monarch, Queen Elizabeth, in grace and staying power. Barak Obama at his second inaugural speech, acknowledged the 'fringe-benefits (A tongue-in-cheek reference to Michelle's new hair-style) of a lawyer wife. She, very unobtrusively, took up socially relevant issues and remains a strong presence. Hillary Clinton displays a mojo that is sparkling.

Indira Gandhi who was dismissed in a chauvinistic phrase as the "*Goongi Gudiya*" made many a man zip-lock their lips with her Durga-like courage. Our current political platform has thrown up some interesting *dramatis personae.* We have a Didi who in her non-elitist avatar is close to the grass-roots. Promoting Rabindra Sangeet by playing it at the traffic intersections in Kolkata she wants to cool the fiery passion of the Bong. Seems to have imbibed the exhortation of 'Ekla Chalo' by snapping ties with whoever challenges her preferring to plough a lonely furrow. But when provoked ready to jump into the fray with '*khela hobe*'. We have an Amma from tinsel town who acquired great political acumen and bargaining power to stay relevant. So much so that she was revered as a '*Puratchi Thalaivi*' (Revolutionary Leader). We have a *Behen ji,* who has learnt to hoist the opposition with its own petard and bag the votes (that too in designer bags). Since we have a Didi, Amma and Behen ji, how can we overlook the '*dharam patni*' from Bihar with the sweetest of names, who bailed her husband out by becoming the Chief Minister to keep the political '*chulla*' burning for him?

Success stories of women from the corporate, literary, social and entertainment arenas abound. So don't let your mind get affected by malware of regressive social conditioning. In a knowledge world where physical prowess alone is not the silver bullet, your biology can be your destiny to rise and shine.

#Me Too & Bye Bye Bikini

A Salute to the New Woman

The hash-tag #Me Too has been snowballing and gathering momentum for more than a year now— a global scream against the predatory male gaze and sexual harassment. Women are shedding their silent victimhood and in a show of solidarity calling out the perpetrators. Sure enough, a slew of powerful moguls have been knocked off their thrones. With all the ignominy attached to him after the #Me Too expose, Weinstein should certainly add the letter s' as a prefix to his name!

In this societal churn, hash-tag #Bye-Bye Bikini has tagged itself onto the ramp of Miss America Pageant. Americans woke up to the news on 'Good Morning America' sometime ago that Miss America pageant had nixed the swimsuit competition. A gaggle of 50 girls from the U.S. of A in skimpy designer bikinis strutting their stuff was always a hot button routine attracting max eye-balls for almost a century! This unceremonious scrapping of the bikini round by this venerable organisation has won a round of applause from the newly awakened woman, who thinks that vital statistics are not the physical attributes but your mindset and social responsibility.

By a strange happenstance the two hash tags trending now have a common link in the person of Gretchen Carlson, a former Miss America herself. She chairs the all female Board of Trustees of Miss America Pageant (now renamed Competition). An early advocate of the #Me Too movement, she is the hunter who caught the fox in his lair two years ago. Roger Ailes, her former employer and the head honcho of Fox News, was exposed by her for sexual harassment and had to step down.

This New Woman is a result of a long battle against male entitlement and blatant patriarchy. Flashback to 1969—a protest by 400 feminists against the Miss America pageant as a 'Degrading Mind-less-Boob-girlie Symbol' and 'The Consumer Con-Game', amongst other accusations, did not yield any immediate results. There was a theatrical bonfire of feminine symbols like bras, mops, false eye-lashes etc. at the Atlantic City Boardwalk to draw attention to the radical cause. Ironically, things will come full circle in September, 2018, when the new Miss America will be chosen at the same City Boardwalk to celebrate her accomplishments and her talents and her social impact initiatives.

The combo-power of these two hash tag movements promises to reveal a lot more than a bikini does! Besides, Meghan Markle, America's freshly minted royalty, is a staunch supporter of #Me Too movement and women's empowerment causes. Her statement that 'It's time to focus less on glass slippers and more on glass ceilings' asserts her belief in gender equality. The male of the species better learn that it is better to swim with the tide and not against it, with or without swim suits!

***

LOH and LOC

Cross the Line at Your Own Peril

No barbed wires here. Only barbed comments that do the trick. No fences to guard this territory. Yet every household worth its salt has a demarcated Line of Control (LOC) where the Lady of the House (LOH) defends her turf with the zeal of a vigilante. The Man of the House is also not a shrinking violet. So the battle lines are drawn for his and her territory. Any transgressions across the LOC are not only frowned upon but challenged instantly. The territorial warfare on the domestic front can get as embroiled as an international crisis. No composite dialogue will help to defuse the situation. A temporary cease-fire, yes, but the cold war continues till some CBM's (confidence building measures) are brought into play.

In household management, the LOH considers the kitchen as sacrosanct turf. The kitchen protocol according to her stipulates that maids come first and then the spouse. A brilliant concept because the maids have such strategic power these days that even international relations can be 'maid' or marred through the *contre temps* of maids. Indo-US relations have gone from hot to frozen after the recent maid imbroglio at the U.S. Embassy.

The viral popularity of T.V food shows has made the husbands aspirational and demanding. No longer content with the staple *dal-chawal* menu, one is expected to dish up fancy foods a la food-show hostesses Padma Lakshmi or Nigella Lawson. These culinary divas rustle up mouth-watering exotic dishes while looking unruffled and dishy themselves. Get real, chaps! Besides, take the cue from the fact that the best chefs in the world are the male of the species. So how about rustling up some 'khana khazana' exotica for the Missus?

The LOC bristles with ack-ack fire on the days the maid is AWOL.(Away without official leave) Try asking for assistance in carrying the used dishes to the kitchen sink. You get a sinking feeling at the sight of this Qutub Minar of plates and bowls, a neat Lego tower raised in the sink! Alas! No 'chai pe charcha' in the kitchen cabinet. More likely the LOH is ready to throw in the kitchen towel.

Leaving the cupboards with gaping mouths is an irritant for most housewives, not only those suffering from OCDS (obsessive compulsive disorder syndrome). But the menfolk seem to have imbibed the policy of 'glasnost' (open door) in acting thus. But I leave it to you to judge. It is an open and shut case for a disorderly trait.

The Man of the House has his own Lakshman Rekha. Don't ever try to mess up the pages of the morning stack of newspapers. By the time I get round to reading them, there are gaping windows from wherever the articles have been cut off for cogitation later. We all have our pet peeves, so there!

Another area where the battle of the sexes continues apace is the bathroom, if you do not have the luxury of His and Hers. The western style loos where friction over whether the toilet seat should be up or down can cause more than a wrinkle in conjugal relations. Some gents bathe in a fashion to make the washroom look as if an elephant has had a bubble bath in there. Alas! One may have to admit defeat in this battle of Waterloo. Well you win some, you lose some.

Men are from Mars and women from Venus, an apt observation. Come to think of it, according to a recent newspaper report, a ticket for a one way trip to Mars is a feasibility by 2024! Any takers?!

***

Air Wives' View

Those Magnificent Men in their Flying Machines

From the groves of academe to the world of the Air Force was a bit of a culture shock. As a bride, I became a part of the Services family more than two decades ago. The crew-room buddy-talk and the cryptic lingo which these men bandied about seemed like gobbledygook to me. This jargon rolled off the tongues of senior wives with equal ease. As a new entrant I felt like the proverbial new kid on the block and was stumped by the abbreviations used, which to my uninitiated ears sounded like chemistry formulae. The CO and the COO were neither pigeons on an amorous sortie nor gaseous emissions, but a powerful combine of the Commanding Officer and the Chief Operations Officer. Compared to this Einstein's theory of relativity seemed more familiar.

Brought up on a diet of English Literature, the Services jargon seemed a different kettle of fish. One learnt a whole new 'vocab' regarding the uniforms and the trappings that go with these for different occasions. Epaulettes Ribbons, Wings, Aiguillettes, Lanyards, Miniature and Ceremonial Medals, Cummerbunds etc. remain the order of the day for the spit and polish routine of parades and ceremonials. That the flier-boys had an impish humour became apparent to me soon enough when an officer referred to as 'Tiny' turned out to be a strapping six-footer.

Having had a ringside view of the Air Force for more than two decades, I can't help admiring the dedication and the zest for life these men exhibit. What really won me over was the openness and warmth with which one was accepted into the fold. The rites of passage from Civvy Street to the Services world were painless indeed. The wives, over a period of time, tune into the Air Force ethos with equal commitment. They form the underpinning of the emotional support system. The motto of the Air Force Wives Association (AFWWA), "Vayu Shakti Sangini'— literally meaning a consort of the men with Air Power— is certainly apt.

The AFWWA sorority provides the right ambience in which wives are exposed to Air Force culture and learn to appreciate its nuances. Despite an itinerant lifestyle, the wives carve out suitable careers, enriching their own lives and that of the Services family at large. As someone jokingly said that the contribution of wives gives Air Force two for the price of one!

Behind the glamour of the Service uniform and Mess parties lies a world of solid camaraderie, professionalism and discipline that is unbeatable. These strong bonds are forged through sharing life, close encounters with death in war and peace and togetherness in good and bad times. A new chapter began with the induction of women into most branches of the Air Force, adding more feathers to the service cap. The Air Force is indeed a way of life, a way of thinking— a microcosm of true secularism —the quintessence of the idea that is India. A Srini from Kanyakumari, a Parvez Rathar from Kashmir, a Deshu from Kandla, a Baruah from Kamrup and many more from this varied land of ours, all shape up into officers and gentlemen, and gentlewomen too, for whom the sky is the limit.

***

Ma Tujhe Salaam

Angels on Earth

I am not a feminist Godzilla but as part of the 'womanity' that holds up half the sky I must echo Bob Dylan's words: 'times they are a changin'! Manu muddied the waters centuries ago with his patriarchal edict that 'women are like property on which only the owner has absolute powers'! Whereas the other extreme of women being worshipped as Goddesses was also over the top! Many walls in Indian homes were and are still adorned with Raja Ravi Varma's calendar art in cheap prints showing Saraswati, Lakshmi and other mythological characters.

Even in mythology one can see a gender bias if you ask me, or even if you don't! Gods are multi-headed and multi armed but Goddesses are only multi armed, never multi headed! This visualisation has perhaps surreptitiously leached into attitudes towards women. Lord Rama who holds sway over the Indian minds and hearts till today was hailed as *'Uttam Purush'*—an ideal man. And yet he asked Sita to prove her chastity after *Ravana* kept her in confinement. I have yet to hear of an instance in history where a man is exiled or chastised for being unchaste on mere suspicion!

Perhaps not based on fact as evidenced by the British Museum, the idea of the Chastity Belt with a padlock in Europe seems to be the product of a prurient male imagination of controlling the female sexuality. Even worse practices of female sexual mutilation adopted in some African and Asian countries persist to this day. Not to forget female foeticide in our own Bharat Ma!

The silver lining is that Gen Z is not burdened with this baggage. Baby boomers and the preceding generations were caught in a cleft. Not these 'cool' kids who are a whole alphabet ahead of the oldies in more ways than one! They can handle any manifestation of gender in any combo of alphabet—LGBTQ! They have reinforced the concept that Mother is a dimension, not just a female form!

Mothers cannot be defined but felt! Love for mother transcends class, race, age and gender. What a fine construct a Mother is! Even as adults whenever in distress, we in India say, *'Hai Ma'*! It is only when we express shock and awe that we say, *'Bap Re Bap'*! An umbilical bond that stays alive even after being sundered.

A steel magnolia who can unplug drains and minds; cook up a storm in the kitchen (of course, there is always Zomato!) and unleash a tsunami of ideas in the boardroom, work with grit and determination and yet melt into tears at the sight of a hurt child, animal or bird. She can be a gale force of Nature and a gentle breeze too. She is Aditi, Mother Earth, Shakti: she is all this and much more! No single celebratory day, least of all a commercialized Mother's Day promoted by the likes of Archie cards, can encompass the gratitude we owe to all Mothers.

On this Mother's Day and every other day one should marvel at the toughest job in the world executed with such grace. I will fall back on Bollywood lyricists and composers who unfailingly create lilting songs for every occasion in life. So with a nod of acknowledgement to A R Rehman, I say '*Ma Tujhe Salaam*'!

✷✷✷

The Nude Dude

The Sultan of Seduction

Yes, Ranveer, is on a 'Break the Internet' roll, a la Kim Kardashian who did a photo shoot in 2014 for the same indie magazine, *Paper,* with 'Break the Internet' cover issue. And it did! Kim K was *au naturel,* not kicking butt — but showing hers in full glory.

Now Ranveer, the *enfant terrible* that he can be, has unleashed a tug-of war on social media over his nude spreads on a fine oriental carpet — that is if any one notices the carpet.

The puritanical 'nay sayers' (mostly males!) are not merely raising their eyebrows but spouting a fusillade of angry comments, some downright obnoxious. The women whose modesty Ranveer is supposed to be outraging are delighted with his maiden 'dare to bare' act. It is bruited that Ranveer's Begum Deepika Padukone, a star in her own right, gave him 'permission' to do the photo shoot and then splash it on social media. If it is true, a great comment on 'woman power'! The unstoppable Vidya Balan's comment on feasting her eyes on the nude hunk has earned her an army of trolls. Another instance of the 'new woman' fearless in expressing her opinion. Only if the patriarchal attitude gets erased slowly by sensitising the males on gender equality.

But ask these self-righteous trolls if the male gaze on a woman's body is acceptable, why not the other way round? Curiously enough, when a woman wants to cover her body with a '*burkini*' on the beach instead of showing skin in a bikini, she has to fight for her rights to be clad! Under the veneer of being modern and progressive, there lurks a Victorian sensibility in most of us that feasts its eyes on the red hot magazines in private but its public face upticks only 'kosher' stuff.

The man in the buff is perhaps nudging this masquerading mass to understand that to be truly 'with it', it is better to be 'without it'. Ranveer as a male is a breath of fresh air. Ironically enough, he raises hackles even when he is clothed! Far from being a conservative dresser, his mix of colours and styles in apparel is bizzare to some. He gets the thumbs up from the millennials, who are used to more fluid categories. They enjoy the quirky combos he wears and carries off with a flamboyance that is endearing.

A few folks have filed an FIR against Ranveer for indecent and obscene behaviour ever since Insta caught fire with his photo shoot pics. These affronted souls are perhaps running scared that Ranveer being the 'Badshah of Bollywood' would set in motion an avalanche of admirers in copycat acts of going unclad. Despite this kind of trolling gathering momentum against an artistic photo shoot, no fears that Ranveer will turn into the 'Bad'-Shah' of Bollywood!

This act is, actually, a symbolic twist to the Danish writer Hans Christian Anderson's folk tale 'The Emperor's New Clothes'. In the original story the Emperor's vanity lets him believe that he is wearing a gossamer thin attire, when he is actually naked. But this Emperor of Bollywood with a cool smouldering stare and a statuesquely sculpted body knows that he is naked.

The Sultan of Seduction obviously believes that sexual hypocrisy should be shed. Just as there are mic-drop moments, this is a clothes- drop moment!

✸✸✸

Who is Afraid of Management Gurus?

Wonder Woman

It is a truth universally acknowledged that nerdy management types graduating from the portals of Ivy League institutes are deserving of genuflections from us all! Their 'high falutin' jargon wraps itself around our heads and we are gobsmacked by their weighty pronouncements.

After a lifetime of household management done without a fancy salary or fanfare, unlike the corporate whiz kids with fat wallets, some gutsy women finally reached a tipping point. And one could hear the shattering sound of the shards falling from the glass ceiling as women took to the public space and still handled the home portfolio.

Patriarchy, dented and bruised with this jagged shower, has had to rejig itself considerably. Though even now in many pockets of the world toxicity raises its head by berating women for wearing revealing attire or not wearing attire mandated to keep the women in thrall. Sadly, women are being killed for asserting their agency! To dress as they please, stay at home or work outside or use the post-Covid convenience of work from home aka WFH. It is regressive to behave as if we are still in the troglodyte phase of civilisation with man being the hunter-gatherer and the woman a stay-at -home care giver.

Gone are the days when one was admonished with, 'Remember who wears the pants?' This is no longer valid as genders are as fluid as clothes and hairstyles! The Gen- X has sloughed off the old rigid beliefs fortunately.

Instead of being total acolytes of these founts of wisdom, women's own strategising in public or home space is in a super league, worthy of emulation. My first quibble is with the word 'management' itself! Why not a gender neutral word? There is a clutch of management maestros of modern times whose strategies are oracular in tone.

A scintillating galaxy of management Gurus, with stellar names like Peter Drucker– the Bhishma pitamah of management thinking, C.Northcote Parkinson, CK Prahlad of the 'core competence' catch word, Bill Gates and Steve Jobs– the digital dragons–. Nassim Taleb of 'The Black Swan Moment' fame, Warren Buffet–the Wizard of Omaha–and happily also a clutch of women influencers shine on the marquee. Many of these thought leaders become philanthropists after amassing fortunes that would please even the Croesus doppelgänger, Kuber. But women always believed that charity begins at home.

Randomly, take C. Northcote Parkinson's pithy management law: "Work expands so as to fill the time available for its completion". He, obviously, was an armchair thinker who never encountered a hardworking housefrau. If he had, he would've modified his law to read 'Work expands endlessly so as to fill the shrinking time for its completion'.

Women have the soft skills of empathy, communication and net working in the real sense, learnt in the high voltage battleground called a household. One would do well to learn from this multitasking biped human wonder called the housewife and from women in general who have apparently a 'brahamastra' in that double X chromosome. Maybe a new Algebra is called for where XX=XY.

***

Wordsmiths: Trending Vocab

FOMO
LOL
MASK
VACCINE SHOT
COVID
WFH
ZOOM-BOOM
LOCKDOWN

Anatomy of a Middle

Not This, Not That

I have harboured a secret desire to write a 'Middle' since aeons. Somehow I feel the time is ripe to attempt it now. Having crossed the fiftieth milestone of my life I may be sliding into dotage but then I am also into 'anecdotage'. The former carries with it a likelihood of making me 'muddle-headed' but the latter is certainly an asset for the 'middle-minded'. But before putting pen to paper I thought it prudent to test the waters with my family- my immediate and very vocally critical audience. by saying, "Mom, should n't you just write the beginning and the end, perhaps the middle will take care of itself". Cynicism is the prerogative of the youth, so what can one say!

Not one to be put off by irreverent remarks I thought of seeking a second opinion on my literary malady from someone closer my age. "Don't you have anything better to do than indulge in middlebrow activities?" promptly shot back my better half. The family was certainly having a field day punning at my expense. I should have thought writing middles would be an ideal preoccupation for the middle-aged! Such a volley of tongue-in-cheek comments put paid to any further spot surveys by me on my Hamletian predicament of "To be or not to be– a writer of middles!"

I pondered over this word-construct that goes under the rubric of a 'Middle'– because of its position on the editorial page. A devoted coterie of readers considers their day incomplete without having read the day's piece. Rubbing shoulders with alarming global issues it still maintains a calm countenance. Whether it is personal, general, anecdotal or philosophical, a gossamer tension holds it together. These are words that bring a smile to one's lips, hearty laughter at times, and occasionally a sentimental piece causes a lump in your throat and brings tears to your eyes. A slice-of- life with a distinctive individual stamp. The words flow from minds nurtured in the rich traditions of our land. This creates a subtle bonding with the writers and for this alone the middle should be accorded a special status in the lexicon of literary terms.

Having analysed what makes a middle tick, I was getting cold feet wondering if I had the wherewithal to create something print-worthy. To get a foothold in the world of middles one has to write a piece that can hold the reader's attention from start to finish. No mean achievement that! But before it can see the light of the day it has to pass muster under the gimlet eye of the editor.

Like the Supreme Editor who puts a full-stop to our existence whenever He chooses, the editor of the 'Middle Kingdom' exercises a similar power over the fate of the writer of middles. It is the dustbin or the printed page. However, despite the barbs about my middle-mania and my own nagging thoughts, I decided to take the plunge. Suddenly I have developed an aversion to collecting my mail. Rejection slips have a way of finding their way into letterboxes. From the recesses of my mind pop up lines from Robert Frost- *"We run round a circle and suppose / The secret sits in the middle and knows"*. I can only sigh and wait!

The Middle Path

The Lure of Name and Fame

Words are a tease. More so the right ones. They seem like wispy feathers that fly away at the slightest gawky touch. One has to cajole, caress and approach them gently. Having coaxed elusive words into some shape for publication as well as clearing the hurdle of editorial scrutiny for the first time, I remember the sheer joy of seeing my piece—what's called a 'middle' in journalistic parlance—in a crisp morning newspaper. I waited patiently one full day for some feedback. Not a single call of appreciation from family or friends!

So it was time to take the matter into one's own hands. I conducted a telephonic opinion poll the next day on my word construct. The very first call dampened my spirits. "What, your article? Oh, I missed it. What name do you write under, incidentally?" queried the cheerful voice at the other end. Was that an innocent question or a Freudian slip, giving away the subconscious attitude of the respondent to my writing? May be one does need to have an alias, an aka, to hide under. Should women writers revert to the Victorian practice of assuming male pseudonyms? A name with a nice macho ring would perhaps do the trick. After all, the mind can run riot and concoct some sonorous male pseudonyms. But gender bias in this day and age didn't ring true.

My next call drew a blank again. "Oh well, I did see the title"' said my friend, "but I was put off by the heading so didn't read it." Well, each to his poison. Another astounding response was, "Oh yes, I read the piece but didn't look at the author's name. Was that by you?" So much for name and fame! Yet another friend was called gingerly, having been bitten twice I was thrice shy! This time there was better luck: "Yes, I really liked your 'middler'." Middler? One wondered whether the synonym for the strange coinage 'middler' was 'howler'. That made the comment very suspect.

I never thought that a simple act of writing some innocent lines would unleash such paranoid tendencies in me.

Dark images of famous writers going off the deep end cropped up in my mind. No wonder the Bard said, "The Poet, the Lover, and the Lunatic are of one imagination compact." But there is solace to be had in the fact that one was not in the same league and didn't have a reputation to lose. Getting a grip on myself, I therefore persisted with my tele-poll. My next victim was a good friend given to puns and light reading. To my standard question whether he'd read my Middle, he replied with great relish, "Now, now, I could read your palm, your face, your lips, but reading your middle seems like an interesting proposition."

That put paid to any further quest for appreciation. The newspaper that had carried my piece was consigned to the *'raddi'* heap without a requiem. Looking back on yesteryears when a genteel linguistic style was the order of the day, I had an epiphany. It struck me with force that, to grab eyeballs instantly in these high decibel times one has to use words that hit you in the face.

Notice the fame—or rather notoriety—gained by the innocuous sounding words of the hit song from the movie, Delhi Belly. It seems that the line."Bhag D K Bose" repeated as a looped mantra yields a cuss-word in our colourful vernacular street lingo. Nothing genteel about it. A swear word it is, and it hasn't been ignored or overlooked. In fact, many individuals bearing the same name from our 'bhadralok' community have as a result been basking in their own 15 minutes of fame. One will have to question the saying, "What's in a name?" A lot it seems!

***

English Vinglish

Yeh Dil Maange More

India is certainly the new flavour of the world. Nope, it is not because of the spicy chicken tikka masala and the jalfrazie titillating the taste buds of the gourmands across the globe. What is making waves is India's growing economic prowess –which is being linked to the broad swathe of its English speaking whiz-kids. They are the star-performers twinkling on the global marquee. Though savvy in 'bespoke' English they often speak a tweaked variety of English peppered with words from a babble of tongues in India.

Macaulay's strategy of raising a crop of English speaking 'babus' to run the British Empire may have served its purpose, but as our Southern iconic super star Rajanikanth would say, 'Mind it'! We have now a clear case of Empire striking back through the new Lingua Indica. Our motley crowd of IT poster-boys, management gurus, and financial wizards in top slots of MNC's, are the envy of the world. They flit across the world stage with the natural ease of a ballerina doing a minuet. These go-getters of 'Youngistaan' speak a brand of 'yeh dil maange more' brand of Hinglish. The custodians of 'propah' English have conceded that some of our grammatical gaucherie is acceptable 'angrezi' and we are 'loving it'. Our facility in speaking English has won us the reluctant admiration of even the Chinese who have taken to teaching English en masse in stadiums.

Bernard Shaw's caustic comment that 'England and America are two countries separated by a common language' doesn't perturb our young blades lest a similar charge be levelled against us Indians. Even though the trans-Atlantic linguistic cold war continues apace in terms of idiom and accent, our Indian lads are very comfortable in their skin. 'Hinglish' is their preferred tongue. Their desi English flaunts a masala flavour all its own, as popular as the masala chai from Mumbai to Manhattan. College campuses, the catchy commercials and Bollywood, the language labs for this lingo called Hinglish, have lent a certain zing to this spicy concoction. Realising the importance of learning English as a passport to economic empowerment, the demand for learning the tongue has spread across the social classes.

The young brigade, pretty 'bindaas' in their attitude towards the lingo they use, flaunt a fusion English that doesn't go down too well with the purists of the tongue. What has the lexical conservatives foaming at the mouth is the cult of abbreviation a la texting via SMS through the all-pervading phenomenon called the mobile phone. To them it is extremely 'noying 2 see' a pot-pourri of truncated words with numerals masquerading as alphabet! We may pooh-pooh the thought but perhaps this abbreviated formulaic lingo has a literary lineage. An early instance of 'texting' could perchance be seen in A.A. Milne's book, "Winnie the Pooh". The loveable Eeyore the Donkey's lost tail, found later on the Owl's door, is being used as a bell-pull with the terse notice... 'Ples ring if n nswr is reqird'. Children's literature, yes, but certainly a harbinger of the current SMS-ese! To give a proper pedigree to the practice of abbreviations, one can go to the literary maestro who set the fiction-world ablaze with his magic-realism. Salman Rushdie in his book, "Haroun and the Sea of Stories" uses the same texting technique in this compressed phrase -P2C2E-(Processes too complicated to explain). Jacques Barzun's comment, 'Simple English is no one's mother tongue. It has to be worked for', could be altered and adapted as the motto for this new brand of the English language. Whether it is English proper, American English or 'Hinglish', or for that matter Pidgin English, the fact remains that English has a new avatar— it is known as 'Globish', a globally spoken tongue! The latest feather in the Hinglish cap is that the Oxford English Dictionary has officially accepted the word "Aiyoh"! 'Jai Ho', is all we can say!

***

Trending Vocabulary

B.C to P.C.

"When I use a word", Humpty Dumpty said in rather a scornful tone, it means just what I choose it to mean—neither more nor less". In Lewis Carroll's charming fable "*Through the Looking Glass*" Alice is flummoxed by this uber cool statement made by the nursery rhyme immortal. Those of us caught in the crosshairs of this tech-tonic shift feel lost like Alice while the Gen-next is laughing out loud (LOL) at our bewilderment on the new cyber-speak.

Instant mobile connectivity has created an embarrassment of riches by way of smartphones and other gadgetry. We need to re-boot our minds to figure out a virtual wonderland of words and apps. It is a grab-bag of buzz words, trending quotes, viral videos and what have you that has the cyber junkies in its thrall.

The haves and the have-nots have morphed into a knowledge divide of Gen.

B.C. (Before Computers) and Gen.P.C. (Post Computers). And the B.C.'s are in dire need of vocab rehab as they suffer from PTSD (Post technology stress disorder). A whole new parallel world of netizens and other quaint cyber-species has emerged. Don't fly off the handle if asked

'What's your handle?' If you are not part of the Twitterati you could be a silly twit. Not LinkedIn—no way to be. The social networking addicts look askance at you for not being a Face- booker and posting messages on the wall. All this is enough to drive the oldies up the wall.

In the days of yore the innocent pleasure in building one's word-prowess through the printed word was enough. There was always good old Wilfred Funk of Reader's Digest fame challenging us with his regular feature, "It Pays to Increase Your Word Power." We memorised the vocab diligently. But now online search engines, the new cyber genies working almost at nano speed, answer your queries at the click of a mouse. Keeping up with the times, even the venerable Encyclopaedia Britannica has sloughed off its mortal coils preferring to assume an online avatar. A cyber nirvana of sorts!

Some viral words and phrases glide into the Hall of Fame and some slide into the Hall of Shame. Cricket lovers would know about the cricket scams that had spot-fixers in a fix. 'Slapgate' and the earlier 'Monkeygate' fracas involving an Aussie player were viralwords with an underpinning of risqué humour. Who can ignore the current belle of the word-world:'post-truth?' Along with 'alternative facts' this combo has America totally in a twist. To quote Francis Bacon, "What is Truth? said Jesting Pilate and would not stay for an answer."

Before the advent of the internet we too had catchy phrases like Nehru's 'tryst with destiny' but there was no instant cyber circulation. Our Bombay cinema with its respectable pedigree of hundred years has given us innumerable trending phrases on its own steam. "Mere Paas Maa hai" and Gabbar's pithy "Kitney Aadmi They", amongst many more, still retain their mojo.

Vocab has not only been tweaked but shrunk with the SMS unleashing texting as a way of life with the digitally fixated generation. Well, the subtext is that spellings no longer cast a spell as words are truncated and abbreviated into skeletal entities. With digital addiction even amongst the very young, one has to beware of the perils of this brave new world. The attention deficit syndrome has led to serious literature being read in the SMS texting format for those in a hurry. Last heard Shakespeare's "Romeo and Juliet" was blasphemously subjected to this Procrustean exercise. Many wannabe writers cater to this niche of Quick Reads.

Those of us long in the tooth, caught on the cusp of this technology upheaval, have to take a leaf out of Salman Rushdie's book "Haroun and the Sea of Stories". A wizard with words and way ahead of the texting dudes– Rushdie would say these are P2C2E (Processes too complicated to explain!)

***

Quo Vadis Lingua Anglicus

Many Avatars of the English Tongue

Many an eyebrow would certainly be raised at this high brow stringing of Latin words in this age of abbreviated and Procrustean English used by the texting generation. So here is *mea culpa* at the outset for the title!

You can safely say it is Latin or Greek to you because you would be right—it is Latin! The facts testify that English still retains a great deal of its pedigreed ancestry with a closet full of Latin phrases. Jurisprudence, for instance, would be bereft without its Latin terminology. Not to be de-robed completely Lingua Anglicus retains its Latin connect for the sake of gravitas.

Brought up on an addictive diet of SMS's and cyber bites, the Gen next particularly has a decided distaste for 'a farrago of words' (Due apologies to Shashi Tharoor!) The sharpening of the attention deficit syndrome by the lure of the flickering image and the weakening of the reading habit has almost dethroned what used to be a storied Grammar book by Wren and Martin. A comprehensive guide for native and foreign students of the English tongue and a Bible for generations of students and Grammarians.

The young do not play by the old grammar rules. They make their own. Capital letters can be dropped with ease and now the poor apostrophe is also being jettisoned. Some interesting changes are the modified pronouns to indicate gender neutral usage. Spellings are changed to shed any redundant letters in the word. Anyway why learn spellings when Google and predictive text can give you the answer. Though predictive text can make you blush occasionally because Artificial Intelligence (AI) can be mechanical and unmindful of the context at times. The resultant sentence can be hilarious or even awkward.

The parallel universe of social media is more real to the new generation. Speed in tapping on the keyboard and limitations on the number of characters to be used on some microblogging platforms has led to the devising of a whole set of abbreviations and an arcane vocabulary. FOMO (Fear of missing out, in case you belong to the old school of English) rules supreme in their mercurial mind space. Numerals and alphabet are coalesced to form a word. 4get the old strai8 jacket of alphabet alone! Now alphabet is adorned with emojis or emoticons. The lonely exclamation mark must be exclaiming in sorrow at being knocked off the pedestal by the emojis come lately. But then the emojis are so much more glitzy and have the mojo to be eye catching! Witness the popularity of Snapchat.

Yet it is a pertinent question—Where is the English tongue headed? It certainly is at the top of the English linguistic pop-chart in terms of usage and snob value. Being the language of the internet, it does have a clear edge on others staking a claim to the No.1 slot. Though our euphonious Sanskrit, supposedly more refined than Greek or Latin, with its perfect grammar could've been ideal for the internet age if it had been a spoken language. It survives as a ceremonial language for rituals in India.

The reason for the ascendancy of English is because of its open hearted embrace of words from other languages and cultures it came in contact with. The Brits have a whole cachet of Anglo-Indian vocabulary encapsulated in the famous glossary 'Hobson-Jobson' by Henry Yule.

IMBH (In my humble opinion) Lingua Anglicus will evolve with the flow and wear a mantle that is most suitable for the times. No need to file a 'habeas corpus' petition against the uber smart millennials for the resurrection of Ye olde English! They may just turn around and say O.K. Boomer!

Mind Your Language

The Power of Words

The title above has no connection with the eponymous British sitcom of the late Seventies. With a gaggle of immigrants learning 'English as She is Spoke', the sitcom had more than its share of racial stereotypes. This particular diktat to mind the uttered words is up close and personal.

This is the recent kerfuffle in our parliament— the boiler room that fires the engine to keep the 'Ship of Democracy' ship-shape and afloat. Lok Sabha, a fine collective of political reps from our wondrously diverse nation was the *mis-en-scene o*f a tug-of-war between the opposition and the government on the issuance of a booklet that lists words declared 'unparliamentary' and not to be used in the hallowed halls of the Lok Sabha and Rajya Sabha.

Keeping in mind that fiery debates lead to tempers shooting northwards and the result is vitriolic language, some restraints have to be in place to put the kibosh on unparliamentary language. There were lists earlier too and objectionable words were always expunged from the record. With the list going digital, its easy transmissibility like the Corona virus, has raised the hackles of some word lovers and orators in parliament.

They say malicious intent is being read into innocuous words. What's a debate without a quiver full of unusual adjectives and figures of speech? Shashi Tharoor, the ultimate logophile in the parliament has labelled this list as 'indicative' and not 'definitive'. Those not so familiar with their Wren and Martin might need to brush up their grammar.

This battle of words started with an inadvertent remark made by an opposition stalwart, who instead of using the gender neutral word Rashtrapati, used Rashtrapatni for President Murmu. This transgression snowballed from a murmur to a crescendo in parliament. And then adding kindlings to the fire was the list of prohibited words.

One must remember that this iconic Parliament House, now a venerable hundred years old, has been witness to verbal joustings ever since that magical moment when the 'soul of our nation, long suppressed, found utterance' as Nehru said in his rousing 'A Tryst with Destiny' speech. Its walls have echoed with words of mesmerising orators who disarmed the opposition with barbs tipped with humour. A galaxy of gifted speakers from Nehru, Krishna Menon (who made it to the Guinness Book of Records with his speech to the Security Council on Kashmir in 1957), Vajpayee, Ambedkar, Annadurai, Lohia and Laloo Yadav each with a distinctive stamp.

They gave a tongue lashing to each other inside while debating but sat together chatting and sipping chai amicably outside. One wonders if with the parliament proceedings going live, an element of self-conscious 'performance' has crept in— a 'Selfie Syndrome' of playing to the gallery. So this brouhaha will dissipate and the '*nautanki*' (Pardon me, this word is unacceptable in the parliament) will slip into normalcy.

The current salvos flung at each other, combined with the decibel commotion, bring to mind the graceful image of the first woman Speaker of the Lok Sabha, Meira Kumar; a diplomat by training, with her angelic smile sweetly chiding the irate M.P's to sit down with the now quotable lines "*Baith Jayiye, prem se boliye*", recently tweeted by the eloquent Mohua Moitra in the current ruckus over the list.

Parliamentarians who are familiar with Wilfred Funk's column, 'It Pays to Increase Your Word Power' needn't get into a funk, because it always does. Ask Shashi Tharoor!!

***

The Wizardry of Words

Casting a Spell

In the beginning was the Word and it was divine according to Gospel. Over the millennia words have lost their divinity in the spiritual sense, for sure, but we still have the magical use of words in prose and poetry of literatures around the world. This world of imagination is made possible through the use of words in a unique uncliched manner.

Growing up in Kashmir we had the distinct advantage of hearing and speaking four languages. Kashmiri, Hindi, Urdu and English.

Kashmiri, with its evocative phrases, interesting phonetic cadences plus and a rich vocabulary bank of words from a smorgasbord of Central Asian languages, Persian, Dardic and Sanskrit nurtured us— like a mother tongue always does. Urdu that we heard spoken around, like Hindustani spoken in other parts of India, enriched us with the lyrical Ghazal, Rubai and the finesse of Urdu poetry. And one can never forget the part played by languages in rousing in us the pride of being a Hindustani.

Allama Iqbal in Urdu

— *Saare jahaan se accha Hindustan hamara* — swelled our hearts with pride.

But the line that turns the knife in one's hearts now is:

Mazhab nahin sikhata apnon se bair karna,

Hindi hain hum,

Watan hai, Hindustan hamara!

Down South in India, there were sterling poets like Subramanian Bharati and other regional ones who wrote to kindle that fire in Indian hearts to seek freedom no matter what the cost.

It Is remarkable that the only nation in the world to gain independence by weaponising non-violence (sounds like an oxymoron) was India!

We need more voices like Iqbal and Gandhi to darn the torn fabric of Hindustan into the rich tapestry that it always has been despite being colonised. The innate strength and beauty of the Indian soul has to be revived fully by words that are equivalent to its divine connotation.

An 'India Shining' without any biases in terms of colour, cast, creed, region, gender has to be choreographed in a more complex world now! It is all enshrined in the Constitution. Not such a tough ask?

***

In Gratitude

In pole position for my huge thanks are Kapil, my husband, and Swanzal & Himaal, our twin daughters, for always being a cocoon of support and egging me on to keep my imagination untethered. Also for not rolling their eyes at my constant word-play! Special *gracias* to Kapil for his redoubtable skill in fine tuning this book.

My book would not be the same without Shailendra Singh's amazing sketches. An architect by day and an illustrator by night, Shail's deft lines convey the essence of each piece and pack in subtle humour too. So thankful that he made time to do these despite his busy schedule. He is currently creating a graphic novel set in 12th century India titled, 'KARMA: The Ghosts of Time', with exquisite hand drawn sketches.

To Sanjay Kak, my nephew, an acclaimed documentary maker and author, my gratitude for his publishing '*gyan*' in serial What'sApp messages and detailed emails laced with humour. I have to thank him for teaching me the quirky word 'dingbat'. As a wordsmith I now flaunt it freely.

Diba Mushtaq, the daughter of our dear neighbour in Kashmir, showed total readiness to do a sketch in the midst of mounting a solo exhibition of her paintings in Kashmir. A fine instance of the deep bonds we share in the valley.

I have to acknowledge my debt to the redoubtable Jug Suraiya of *The Times of India* for my debut appearance in print in the 'Middles' space on the edit page decades ago. That set me on the 'write' path! *Merci beau coup!*

Immensely thankful to my friends who took the trouble of reading the book amidst their busy schedules and giving me a good chit on the blurb!

Finally, my appreciation to the dynamic and friendly publishing team at Notion Press, Chennai, for its professionalism in giving the book an attractive physical avatar.

www.ingramcontent.com/pod-product-compliance
Lightning Source LLC
La Vergne TN
LVHW091310150826
845673LV00006B/1605